HIDDEN UNEMPLOYMENT

HIDDEN UNEMPLOYMENT

Discouraged Workers and Public Policy

Terry F. Buss and F. Stevens Redburn

PRAEGER

New York
Westport, Connecticut
London

Library of Congress Cataloging-in-Publication Data

Buss, Terry F.
    Hidden unemployment : discouraged workers and public policy /
    Terry F. Buss and F. Stevens Redburn.
        p. cm.
    Bibliography: p.
    Includes index.
    ISBN 0–275–92612–5 (alk. paper)
    1. Disguised unemployment—United States. 2. Disguised
unemployment—Government policy—United States. I. Redburn, F.
Stevens. II. Title. III. Title: Discouraged workers.
    HD5708.75.U6B87 1988
331.13'704—dc19   88–11760

Library of Congress Catalog Card Number: 88–11760
ISBN: 0–275–92612–5

First published in 1988

Praeger Publishers, One Madison Avenue, New York, NY 10010
An imprint of Greenwood Publishing Group, Inc.

Printed in the United States of America

The paper used in this book complies with the
Permanent Paper Standard issued by the National
Information Standards Organization (Z39.48–1984).

10 9 8 7 6 5 4 3 2

TO THE SISTERS OF THE HUMILITY OF MARY

CONTENTS

TABLES AND FIGURES

TABLES

FIGURES

PREFACE

Sometimes a familiar face, seen in a new light, takes on a strange aspect. Sometimes an old familiar problem turns, on fresh examination, into something unexpected, with unanticipated implications.

In the course of our research and writing on the problem of discouraged workers, we have had this kind of experience. Many of our expectations were shattered and rearranged. The limited previous evidence about this group and what they need or want took on a changed significance when placed in the context of new information from national and local surveys. Several times we were led to reconstruct our categories and suggest new, more appropriate labels for those on the fringes of the labor force.

While the topic may seem to be a rather narrow one—traditionally of interest to a relatively small number of labor-market specialists and policymakers—we think that an analysis of this group may provide keys to understanding several questions of much broader interest. Possibly the most important of these questions is how to design cost-effective programs to help those wanting to work to avoid dependency and be fully productive participants in the mainstream economy. A great deal of what we say about discouraged workers and ways to help them can be applied directly to the problem of welfare reform.

Readers should note that we have undertaken this inquiry as individuals, not as representatives of any institution or agency. The views and opinions expressed here are ours alone, and we bear the responsibility.

ACKNOWLEDGMENTS

This study would not have been possible without the support and encouragement of Dixie Sommers, director of Labor Market Information at the Ohio Bureau of Employment Services, and Dee Roth, chief of Program Evaluation and Research at the Ohio Department of Mental Health. Their efforts are greatly appreciated.

A large part of the research on which this book is based was funded by three agencies in Ohio: the Task Force on Unemployment Compensation, the Ohio Department of Mental Health, and the Ohio Board of Regents Urban University Program. Indeed, Ohio leads the nation in funding public policy research. We are proud to be a part of this effort.

In carrying out the research reported here, the authors were aided by an unusually qualified and dedicated team at the Youngstown State University Center for Urban Studies, who produced and analyzed high-quality data rapidly and efficiently. Special thanks go to Julie DeGalan for processing the data, conducting case-study interviews, and managing several projects, and to George Garchar for managing the entire operation.

Judith Ferrett deserves special mention for her skilled management of the manuscript production process. The final work on the manuscript was accomplished at St. Elizabeth Hospital Medical Center (SEHMC) in Youngstown, Ohio.

Sister Susan Schorsten, H. M., director of SEHMC, and W. Robert Kennedy, director of Medical Education of SEHMC, provided access to data analysis and clerical support at their Educational Research and Development Center. Without their generous contribution, this project could not have been completed.

We particularly are indebted to two premier policy analysts—Roger Vaughan, president of Roger Vaughan Associates, and Bruce Klein of the U.S. Bureau of Labor Statistics—who devoted a great deal of time to reviewing and criticizing various drafts of the manuscript, resulting in numerous improvements. For the flaws and weaknesses that remain, the authors take full responsibility.

Finally, we would like to thank Jim Dunton, economics editor at Praeger. We appreciate his patience and support in bringing the manuscript to publication.

PART I
BACKGROUND

1 THE DISCOURAGED WORKER PROBLEM

Few public issues excite such controversy as that of why so many people in the United States remain unemployed when the nation is creating record numbers of jobs. The issue was raised once again early in 1986 when President Reagan and House Speaker Tip O'Neill exchanged heated words (Healy 1986). The president expressed his belief that many unemployed people did not really want to work, citing that so many jobs were available yet remained unfilled. The Speaker rejected the implication that many unemployed people are lazy or undermotivated, and argued that those who want to work but cannot get jobs represent a huge, unnecessary waste of human capital.

The Reagan–O'Neill controversy crystallizes two sides of an ongoing policy debate: what should government do to promote full employment, to reduce long-term dependency, and to help displaced workers and others who have lost jobs in an ever-changing economy? The key to resolving this debate could lie in a better understanding of those people who stand at the margins of the labor force, that is, between those who demonstrably want to work but cannot, and those who clearly are not interested in working and will not. This book is about one part of that group: those who say they want to work, are ready to work, but do not expect to find work and are not looking for it. These individuals are often called the *discouraged workers*.

Insights regarding discouraged workers also may shed more light on a number of fundamentally important labor-market issues:

- *The changing role of women in the work force*: Women have entered the work force in massive numbers in the last two decades (Gellner 1975). Yet, women are also a majority of discouraged workers.

- *The "feminization" of poverty and development of an "underclass"*: The growth in numbers of welfare-dependent, single-parent female heads of households has drawn increasing attention (Moynihan 1986). Experts have also noted the closely related emergence of an underclass of young males living in urban ghettos and excluded from the mainstream economy.

- *Worker dislocation*: Between January 1979 and January 1984,[1] 11.5 million U.S. workers lost their jobs due to plant closings or relocations, abolition of a position or a shift, or slack work. By the end of this period, 730,000 of these individuals had left the labor force out of discouragement or by retiring earlier than they might have wished (U.S. Congress 1986b).

- *The not-so-poor elderly*: New statistical evidence suggests that the retired elderly are now economically better off, relative to other age groups, than ever before (Murray 1984). At the same time, barriers to the employment of older Americans have been relaxed. Analysis of the elderly who are classified as discouraged workers may help us to understand shifting work incentives and opportunities for the expanding numbers of older Americans.

- *Chronic minority unemployment*: As of 1986, the poverty rate for black Americans was 33.8 percent compared with 11.5 percent for whites. Unemployment for blacks was 16 percent, compared with 7 percent for the overall population. Among black youths, unemployment rates approached 50 percent. Many blacks have only part-time work, and a disproportionate number are employed in low-wage occupations. Analysis of worker discouragement may aid in understanding the tragedy of unemployment in the black community (Wilson 1987).

Discouraged workers are the focus of attention, therefore, both as a subject of interest by itself and as a possible key to gaining an understanding of broader issues. As it turns out, a great deal of what can be said of discouraged workers applies to other groups (i.e., those who want jobs but are not discouraged, according to the U.S. Bureau of Labor Statistics) that stand on the margins of the economic mainstream.

BACKGROUND

Official unemployment statistics are the most watched economic indicators. States and communities measure their economic vitality by them. The federal government uses the unemployment rate in many of its funding formulas for distributing development grants and loans to localities and for distributing training funds and other benefits to individuals. Policymakers and administrators at all levels of government use the rates to judge how well programs reach people in need or to justify new programs. Federal administrators monitor national rates to guide national monetary and fiscal policy. For the unemployed individual, an increase in the official rate can extend the receipt of unemployment benefits beyond the normal 26-week period, but also may signal gloomy prospects for finding work.

Despite their widespread use, many experts question how well official unemployment rates reflect the relative well-being of different localities (cf. Vietorisz et al. 1975 and Buss 1986b). In part, the issues are technical. To be counted officially as unemployed, a person must be not only jobless but also ready, willing, and able to work, *and* be actively seeking employment. Those wanting jobs but neither working nor looking for work are not considered unemployed and, therefore, are officially *not in the labor force*. If many people want jobs but have stopped searching, then a low official unemployment rate will not fully reflect their distress. This discrepancy would be more likely to arise where job prospects have been very weak for a very long time. People are probably more likely to give up looking for work in an economically depressed area. These unemployed people who are not reported in official statistics are sometimes referred to as the *hidden unemployed*.

The Hidden Unemployed

Eliminating people who are not actively seeking work from the total count of unemployed individuals affects perceptions of how well the labor market performs in matching those who want to work with available jobs. In 1984, for example, there was an average of over 8.5 million officially unemployed people in the nation, corresponding to an annual average unemployment rate of 7.5 percent. However, another 6 million adults who professed to want jobs were not working, but were not considered to be part of the labor force. If all those wanting jobs were considered unemployed, the number of people out of work would increase to 14.6 million, and the unemployment rate would rise to 11.4 percent.[2]

Whether to include those wanting work and not seeking jobs in official unemployment calculations has been a subject of controversy since the federal government began its labor statistics program in 1940. On one side, observers argue that, although these people express an interest in working, many are not serious and would not or could not accept jobs if offered. People with children or elderly or disabled dependents to look after, for example, may want a job, but their circumstances prevent them from working. A wage high enough to pay for day care and to yield an income sufficient to justify separation of the child and parent might make the parent a serious job candidate. Others argue that many of the hidden unemployed would work if their prospects looked more promising. They may be prevented from working by a lack of education or job skills, for instance; recognizing this, they have stopped actively looking for work.

On one level, the controversy over these hidden unemployed is a question of values. Should a society concern itself with those who, whether by choice or circumstance, have dropped out of the labor force but still express an interest in working? This question is at the heart of the debate between President Reagan and Speaker O'Neill, who are only the latest debators in a long-standing confrontation over the issue.

Most labor economists would reject both the Reagan and O'Neill views as being too one-sided. They assume that an unemployed person, whether officially counted or not, weighs the income while not working against the expected income from the job he or she is likely to find in the labor market.[3] If the latter exceeds the former by enough to make a job search worthwhile, then the worker will enter or reenter the labor force.[4] A housewife whose husband earns enough to comfortably support the family may not view a job as worthwhile because of day care, housekeeping, or other costs that would offset the financial gain from working. A worker with unrealistic expectations may demand a high salary for low-skilled work at less than 40 hours a week. Not finding any offers, this person does not work. The economically rational behavior predicted in these hypothetical examples can be tested.

Discouraged Workers

Formal economic analysis casts the hidden unemployment issue not as a normative question (i.e., should people behave this way and do they deserve sympathy or not) but as one of labor-market mechanics (i.e., how and why do the ranks of the hidden unemployed swell and shrink with the needs of employers). The main public policy concern of labor economists has been how the existence, size, and characteristics of this reserve pool affect the ability of the economy to handle cyclical and structural fluctuations in labor demand. Economists have assembled some evidence pointing to the conclusion that the hidden unemployed are not an important potential source of labor and do not enter or exit the labor force in sufficiently large numbers to cause extreme expansions or contractions of labor demand (Gellner 1975; Flaim 1984).[5] As a result, they have given only limited attention to the hidden unemployed.

Although labor economists do not view the hidden unemployed as important to the functioning of the labor market, they have observed that when unemployment rates are high, the size of the labor force (i.e., the sum of the employed and unemployed) either shrinks or rises at a much slower rate than when rates are low (Barth 1968). This pattern suggests that when people believe there are jobs available (as evidenced by low unemployment rates),[6] they enter the labor market to search for them. Conversely, when jobs are more scarce (as evidenced by high rates), more people decide not to search for work, perhaps believing that this would be a waste of time. This ebb and flow of workers into and out of the labor force as a function of economic prosperity can be labeled the "discouraged worker phenomenon." It is this group in particular that constitutes the main focus of the analysis to follow.

Discouraged workers, by official definition, are those who express an interest in holding a job but have given up looking for work *because* they either believe that no jobs are available or that they lack the necessary qualifications to get a job. Thus, discouraged workers are a subpopulation of the hidden employed, having given those particular reasons for not seeking work.[7] In 1984, there were, on the average, 1.3 million discouraged workers, amounting to 21 percent of the hidden unemployed, that is, all those wanting work but not actively seeking it. Had just these discouraged workers been included in the national unemployment rate for 1984, the rate would have been higher by 1.1 percentage points, for a total of 8.6 percent.

As part of its statistical program, the U.S. Bureau of Labor Statistics (BLS) gathers limited demographic information about the discouraged worker population. This constitutes most of what is known about discouraged workers. Most are young adults, retired persons, or married women (Wool 1978; Finegan 1978; Job 1979). Together, these three groups comprise the lion's share of discouraged workers.

As with the hidden unemployed, some analysts see discouraged workers as people who are voluntarily unemployed. They believe that most young people in this category—whether high school dropouts or graduates—do not want to work very badly, despite their expressed interest in finding jobs. Similarly, they believe that the retired who are discourged, even if they still have some desire to work, for the most part are not seriously interested. Finally, most of the married women who describe themselves as discouraged are believed to have family responsibilities that tie them to the home.

Other analysts regard discouraged workers as a residual group of unemployed who are less well-qualified than those who have been hired or are actively seeking work. For example, a long-time steelworker who is laid off in a plant closing seeks work but, perhaps because of age or obsolete skills, is not rehired and eventually gives up. In this view, the primary difference between the discouraged worker and those in the labor force is that he or she is not acceptable to employers in the community.

It would be helpful if more attention had been paid by labor economists to resolving these inconsistent views of the discouraged. Instead, as noted, they have been concerned mainly with quantifying the movement of this group into and out of the labor force. Little attention has been focused on who discouraged workers are, how they got that way, and what relationship they have to the labor force (Finegan 1978).

This professional lack of curiosity about discouraged workers would be appropriate if public programs now existed to adequately address their needs or if it had been determined that they are not an important potential source of labor. As an example, if day-care programs were available to most women who want to work for pay but who believe there are no jobs that would let them meet their

Figure 1.1
Labor-Market Definitions

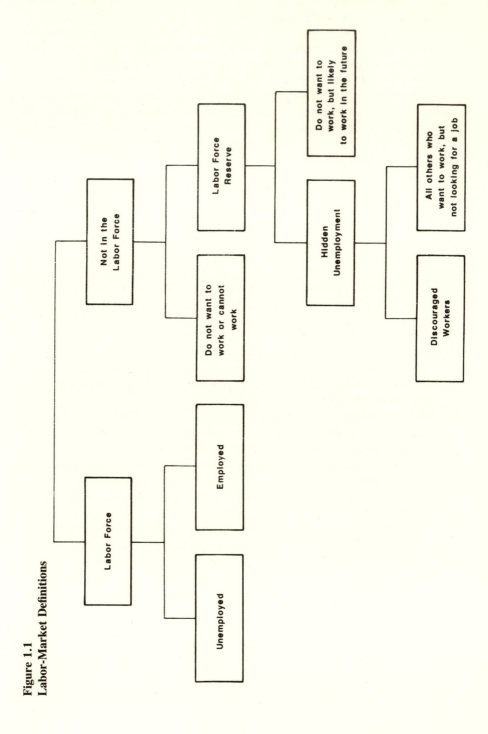

Figure 1.2
Employment Status of U.S. Adult Population, 1984

Total Adult Population

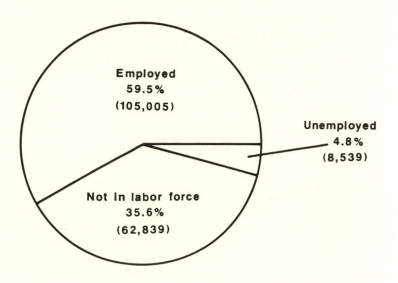

Those not in the Labor Force

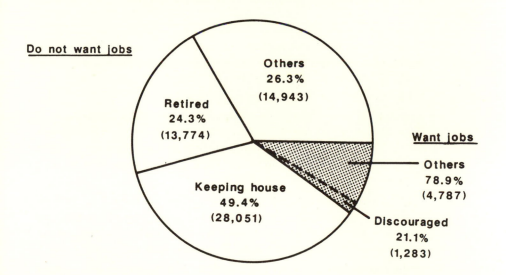

child-care responsibilities, then there would be no need for government action to aid this group. Or, if it were established that the economy benefits from having these women remain at home with their children, despite their expressed desire to work away from home for pay, then perhaps no public effort to help them find employment would be justified. However, it is an open question, first, to what extent discouraged workers need public help to become employed and, second, whether the economy would benefit from their employment enough to justify the cost of this public assistance. The answers to these questions will be crucial in determining what, if any, public policy initiatives are called for to reduce the ranks of discouraged workers.

SOME QUESTIONS OF POLICY

Further research is needed to determine in what ways discouraged workers represent a distinct labor-market group deserving of separate and distinctive treatment. To the extent that discouraged workers resemble others who want to work but are not pursuing jobs, for reasons ranging from family responsibilities to medical problems, on the one hand, or resemble those unemployed but actively looking for work, on the other, then it may be helpful to rethink the current categories.

Data sufficient to address the discouraged worker problem from a public policy perspective have only recently become available. A combination of both published and unpublished data from federal sources and a series of local studies in Youngstown, Ohio, designed to study discouragement, makes it possible to go beyond our previous understanding of this group and its role in the economy.

Among the many basic factual questions that no one has answered previously are these:

- *Work histories and employability*: Do most discouraged workers have extensive work histories or not? Among those who have worked, what kinds of jobs have they held? What skills and experience could they bring to the work force? How employable are they?

- *Means of support*: How do discouraged workers support themselves? How many rely on other household members for income? How many depend on Social Security payments, unemployment insurance, or other public income assistance? What are their financial incentives to seek employment?

- *Finding work*: How many discouraged workers have searched for jobs in the recent past? Did their failure to find work typically result from inefficient methods of searching or from a lack of enthusiasm for the task? Under what conditions would they again look for work?

- *Attitudes toward work and living*: What prospects do discouraged workers see for themselves and their families? How do they regard work itself?

Do they share in the same work ethic that motivates others to seek and hold employment, or not? How do they feel about receiving benefits and services provided by government to the unemployed and discouraged?

* *Psychological status*: How, if at all, is this group's lack of participation in the labor force related to fundamental psychological orientations such as sense of well-being or self-esteem?

* *Change and stability*: Are people typically "discouraged" for long periods, or is this a transitory status? What dynamic underlies the fluctuations in total numbers of discouraged workers that accompanies the business cycle? Is it useful to distinguish between those who have become discouraged workers recently, perhaps after diligently searching for jobs, and those who are chronically discouraged?

These questions are addressed in the chapters that follow. First, in the next chapter, the existing data base about discouraged workers is examined, highlighting gaps in our knowledge and focusing on inconsistencies in the conclusions of previous studies. Then, in chapters 3 through 7, we discuss a more comprehensive profile of the discouraged worker than that which has been available up to now. Going beyond simply demographics, this part of the analysis looks at who they are, how they got that way, what their relationship is to the labor force, and how their presence affects the operation of the labor market under various circumstances. Findings about the discouraged worker are interpreted in the larger context of other current national socioeconomic trends, including the changing nature of poverty, the shifting work roles of women and the elderly, and the accelerated dislocation of experienced workers in manufacturing industries. Chapter 8 summarizes evidence regarding the employment-related needs of discouraged workers. In the book's final chapter, public policies consistent with those needs are outlined.

NATIONAL AND LOCAL STUDIES

The analysis presented in the following chapters draws on data from a series of national studies conducted by the BLS and from four regional–local studies conducted by the Center for Urban Studies at Youngstown State University in partnership with the Ohio Bureau of Employment Services. The regional–local studies were designed (with the cooperation of the BLS and the U.S. Census Bureau) to exactly replicate those by the BLS and, more importantly, were developed to answer many of the questions not addressed in the BLS research program. Combining evidence from both the national and local levels produces a much clearer picture of the discouraged worker than ever before.

Major data sources include the following:

* *National Monthly Current Population Survey*: The BLS, since 1967, has asked questions that identify discouraged workers from a subsample of

those interviewed in the monthly Current Population Survey (CPS) conducted by the Bureau of the Census. This information, published quarterly and summarized annually, forms the basis for comparing selected demographics for discouraged and unemployed workers. It also allows one to compare numbers of workers from the discouraged and unemployed groups over time.

- *National CPS Plant Closing Study—January 1984*: In January 1984, the BLS added a special group of supplementary questions to its standard monthly CPS items (see Flaim and Seghal 1985). These added questions asked whether those surveyed had been involved in plant closings and major job retrenchments from 1979 through 1983. The responses allow one to relate discouragement and unemployment directly to information on plant closings.

- *National Survey of Income and Program Participation—October 1983 to January 1984*: From October 1983 through January 1984, the Bureau of the Census conducted personal interviews nationwide with 20,000 households in the first stage of what will be a continuing national survey. Respondents were asked questions about their employment status, sources of income, and participation in cash and noncash benefit programs (e.g., public housing, low-income energy assistance, and school lunch programs). This new data base provides a detailed picture of how discouraged workers cope with joblessness.

Four studies were conducted in the Youngstown–Warren, Ohio, metropolitan area from 1984 to early 1986 and were intended to replicate and greatly extend the national CPS unemployment surveys:

- *Local CPS Replication—June 1984*: In June 1984, the National CPS Plant Closing Supplement was replicated for a sample of nearly 4,000 people. The local survey followed exactly the procedures and questions used by the U.S. Census Bureau in its national survey (see Buss 1986a).

- *Local CPS Follow-up Survey—Summer 1985*: All discouraged workers and selected others in the 1984 Local CPS Replication survey were reinterviewed in the summer of 1985. At this time, a wide range of employment history, attitudinal, psychological, educational, and other data were gathered. This study was designed to answer many of the major questions about discouragement not answered by the national BLS survey (see Buss and Redburn 1986a).

- *Discouraged Workers Survey—Fall 1985*: Another survey of discouraged workers was undertaken in the fall of 1985 to provide answers to additional questions not already considered in the Local CPS Follow-up Survey.

- *Former Steelworker Study—Summer 1985*: The Youngstown–Warren area was once a world center for steel production. In 1977, one of the largest steel-making facilities, Youngstown Sheet and Tube, permanently shut down, and thousands of workers were laid off (Buss and Redburn, 1983). Workers affected by this shutdown were recontacted in the summer of 1985 as part of a long-term effort to follow impacts of the closing on the area's labor force (Buss and Redburn 1986b). This study applied the BLS definitions and labor economics concepts of displacement. The results can be used to relate the effects of a single plant closing to the National CPS Plant Closing Supplement and to examine the relationship between worker dislocation and discouragement.

DISCOURAGED WORKERS AND PUBLIC POLICY

Constructing a national public policy for discouraged workers requires answers to two questions:

1. Do discouraged workers have distinctive needs that separate them from other groups of nonworking adults, the working poor, and other disadvantaged people—implying the need for public programs addressed specifically to them?

2. To the extent that the needs of discouraged workers are not already met through existing public programs, what policies would address their needs and would be cost-effective, given the potential contribution of this group to the economy through paid employment?

Not only have many labor-market researchers failed to link research findings on discouraged workers with public policy, but also they have failed to link the concept of discouragement, as used in labor economics, with some major recent and ongoing changes in the nation's socioeconomic fabric. We have already noted that studying discouraged workers may lead to a better understanding of current labor-market issues: the changing role of women in the work force, the "feminization" of poverty, the growth of an "underclass," worker dislocation due to shifts in the economy, the not-so-poor elderly, and high rates of chronic unemployment among minorities.

Thus, close examination of the discouraged worker phenomenon should tell us something about other, cross-cutting policy issues of current interest to many people. These issues, addressed in the book's final chapter, demonstrate that the phenomenon of the discouraged worker, which was previously of concern only to academic labor-market economists, may also be a key to understanding several critical problems of interest to a much wider audience.

NOTES

1. Just after our study was completed, the BLS published results from a study of dislocated workers for 1986 (see Horvath 1987), showing that 10.8 million workers had lost their jobs from 1981 to 1986.

2. The higher rate is calculated by adding this group to the labor-force total and to the total of unemployed persons.

3. This expected income is sometimes referred to as the reservation wage (see Feldstein and Poterba 1984).

4. Our example is presented solely in monetary terms for the sake of simplicity. In reality, individuals weigh both monetary and nonmonetary factors.

5. The alternating expansion and contraction of the labor force may be viewed positively or negatively. Generally, negative consequences would accompany the movement of large numbers of people from the "not-in-the-labor-force" category into the ranks of the unemployed; unemployment rates would increase. Generally, positive consequences would result from the movement of those outside the labor force into employment, which would provide workers for job vacancies, and unemployment rates would fall.

6. Individual workers, of course, do not closely monitor unemployment rates as a way of guiding their job-search behavior. Instead, workers may be sensitive to postings of help-wanted signs, published want ads, job listings, and news reports. When information from these sources is positive, workers may begin to look for jobs. Presumably, unemployment rates are a surrogate summary measure of these activities.

7. Other reasons for not seeking a job include: family responsibilities, child care, school attendance, ill health (including physical disabilities and mental handicaps or illness), and lack of transportation, to name a few.

2   *THE EXISTING KNOWLEDGE BASE*

Until the 1960s, most labor economists and policymakers viewed the nation's labor supply as consisting only of those adults who were actually working (the employed) or actively seeking work (the unemployed) (Flaim 1973). People not in the labor force who wanted jobs and had, in apparent futility, given up looking for work, were not considered an important potential source of labor.

In 1962, the Gordon Committee (also known as the President's Committee to Appraise Employment and Unemployment Statistics) began to study the apparent movement of people into and out of the labor force more closely. Because of the hundreds of thousands of people involved, the Gordon Committee concluded that merely separating the working-age population into those who are employed and unemployed versus those who are outside the labor force (i.e., those not officially employed nor unemployed) but wanting jobs was no longer justified, had it ever been (Stein 1967b). This pronouncement brought to the fore the concept of hidden unemployment, including individuals who were labeled, for the first time, "discouraged workers."[1]

Following the recommendations of the Gordon Committee, the U.S. Bureau of Labor Statistics (BLS)—the federal agency charged with compiling employment and unemployment statistics—in 1967 began to collect data on discouraged workers as part of its overall statistical reporting program. This was accomplished by including questions on "discouragement" in the monthly Current Population Survey (CPS)—a nationwide set of personal interviews with about 60,000 households, used primarily to estimate unemployment rates.

These data have been the basis for studies on hidden unemployment. This chapter summarizes findings from these studies and, where possible, updates them with more recent BLS statistics. Out of this review, a multifaceted yet amorphous portrait of the discouraged worker emerges.

HOW DISCOURAGEMENT IS VIEWED

Many explanations have been offered for why people become too discouraged to keep searching for work. In the following discussion, two broad views of discouragement are summarized.

The Conventional View

After two decades of economic transformation and public debate over massive unemployment, the typical discouraged worker has become stereotyped as someone who has worked steadily for most of his or her adult life, but involuntarily became unemployed, perhaps through a plant closing or work-force retrenchment (Flaim 1984, p. 9; Hamel 1979, p. 58). At first searching for work, but lacking marketable skills, too old to be an attractive prospect, and unable or unwilling to move to a community with better work opportunities, the worker finally gives up and relies either on savings, early pension, public assistance, or on relatives or friends. Through all this, however, the worker remains a believer in the work ethic and would work if offered a job. This is the conventional view of discouragement.

A variation on this theme describes discouraged workers as caught by individual circumstances rather than plant closings or general economic distress. Examples include:

- The recent college graduate, who is unable to find work in his or her area of expertise and is overqualified for other occupations, delays entering the job market and continues to live at home with parents or depends on a working spouse.

- The housewife, who no longer has child-rearing responsibilities, tries to reenter the labor force but finds that her skills are unmarketable.

- The convicted criminal, who is often a participant in correctional work-adjustment–transition programs and who has paid a debt to society and developed marketable skills, finds that a criminal record is an impassable barrier to employment and returns to a life of crime.

- Women and minorities, upon encountering discrimination in hiring (Wilson 1987), are unwilling to struggle with legal remedies and abandon the search for work.

- Young people who have dropped out of high school, possibly to get a head start over peers in the work force but more likely because they have become disenchanted with school, find that there are no good jobs in a market biased toward educated and skilled workers (Lerman 1986;

Natriello 1986). Unwilling or unable to return to school, they eventually despair of finding work.

- A person living where work is nearly inaccessible finds it physically impossible to get to a job. Although thousands of new jobs are available in the growing suburbs only a few miles away, many people in the inner city can reach work only with great difficulty or expense, partly because suburban mass transit systems are underdeveloped (U.S. General Accounting Office 1987). The same argument applies to those living in remote rural areas.

- The newly homeless individual, having lost a job and eventually exhausting all resources, ends up on the street or in a shelter. He or she may want to work, but the circumstance of being without a home itself acts as a barrier to landing a job, although not in all cases (see Redburn and Buss, 1986).

- A single parent on public assistance, who wants a job but has few skills and no work experience, finds that welfare is more economically rewarding than work (Domestic Policy Council 1986). After repeatedly failing to find a job that would leave his or her children better off than they are on the public dole, the single parent gives up the search.

Like the discouraged worker of the conventional view, all that separates those individuals just discussed from the unemployed is that the latter have continued to look for work, while the former have given up. Both the discouraged and unemployed want jobs. Those holding the conventional view are inclined to decry the conditions that produce such a waste of human capital (Schweitzer and Smith 1974) and to look for remedies that would bring those people into the labor force.

A Countervailing View

In opposition to this stereotype of the discouraged worker as an available and willing potential participant in the labor force, many labor economists view them as people who are very "weakly attached" to the labor force and thus search for or take jobs only casually and occasionally, if ever (see Finegan 1978; Flaim 1984; Mead 1986; Murray 1984).

Several explanations have been offered for the discouraged worker phenomenon by those who question the conventional view or other prevalent stereotypes. First, people who want jobs but are not looking for work probably have some alternative source of income or support that makes work less attractive—perhaps a parent, spouse, or relative. Also, in many parts of the country, single parents, who have children but lack work experience or adequate skills and education, can receive as much or more income from public assistance programs than they can from working at unskilled, entry-level jobs; thus, they may want a job but would not take any job for which they are qualified.[2] A great deal of research has established that, under these circumstances, public assistance reduces the incentive to work.[3] A not-very-generous welfare system is criticized, ironically, for making not working a financially attractive alternative to holding down a job (Murray 1984).

Second, some people want jobs that conform to a narrow set of personal specifications, such as jobs offering nontraditional hours (e.g., night or split shifts), short or flexible work schedules so that they can pursue other activities, and special (e.g., quiet, dirt or smoke free, or outdoor) work environments. For whatever reason, some people have such restrictive nonsalary criteria for a job that they rarely work.

Third, some people work at jobs that are not counted as valid employment but which allow them to evade taxation (e.g., doing work for cash or barter) or to be paid for criminal activity (e.g., prostitution or drug dealing). By some estimates, these jobs in the "hidden economy" may account for as much as one-third of the nation's income. A more realistic estimate might be 5 percent of the gross national product (GNP) ("The Shadow Economy" 1987). If these underground efforts are really so prevalent, then it may be that many discouraged workers are, despite their response, "officially" employed.

Finally, some people either will not or cannot accept work even if it means living in abject poverty (Mead 1986; Murray 1984). They choose not to work even when decent—although perhaps not glamorous—jobs are available. Some appear to have lost their desire to work. These include the vagabond who has consciously rejected a conventional lifestyle, the alcoholic or drug abuser who cannot cope with the world of work, and those with psychological or emotional problems that keep them from gainful employment. Others may never have worked and, as they become older, lose any expectation of ever working. Street gang members, other poor youths in the nation's ghettos or impoverished rural communities, prodigal sons and daughters of the rich, or single teenage mothers may never enter the labor force.

If workers are discouraged for these reasons, then the so-called "countervailing" view holds, that they do not represent a pool of surplus labor. The probability of larger numbers of discouraged workers entering the labor force is simply too small. More importantly, they do not represent a waste of human capital resources because they will not or cannot work. The cost to society of changing their work status would, in nearly all cases, exceed the value of their potential economic contribution.

These conflicting images of discouraged workers must be resolved if we are to determine the best course for public policy. Are discouraged workers really very like those people who are working or are unemployed but actively seeking work, except that they cannot find jobs and have given up looking? Or, are discouraged workers more like those people who cannot or do not wish to work and, as such, do not constitute a pool of surplus labor that ought to be helped toward employment?

WHAT IS KNOWN ABOUT DISCOURAGEMENT

Even though the controversy about discouraged workers has raged for three decades, we still have only a fragmentary understanding of them (Finegan 1978; National Commission 1979; Flaim 1984). A great deal of our ignorance may be due to the fact that the necessary data have been developed, gathered, and analyzed almost exclusively by and for the U.S. Bureau of Labor Statistics (BLS). As a result, data on the discouraged worker have been useful in answering only a few questions of interest to federal agencies and Congress. Researchers have relied on BLS data rather than designing and executing the kinds of studies that might address a whole range of policy questions about the discouraged worker. Because it has been virtually the only source of knowledge on this subject, an overview of the BLS statistical program is in order.

BLS Statistical Program

The BLS constitutes the only national source of data on discouraged workers. The definitions and procedures used by this agency, and the various national commissions that have been appointed to evaluate them, are critical in developing an understanding of the discouraged worker phenomenon.

The BLS, in partnership with the U.S. Bureau of the Census, conducts a monthly survey, the Current Population Survey (CPS), of more than 60,000 households nationwide to produce employment and unemployment rates and other statistics for the nation and selected states (see U.S. Bureau of Census 1978). As part of this effort, discouraged workers are identified and counted based on answers to the following survey questions:

1. "Has [respondent] been looking for work during the past four weeks?" If respondent answers no, then the next question is answered.

2. "Does [respondent] want a regular job now, either full- or part-time?" If respondent answers yes or maybe, then the next question is answered.

3. "What are the reasons [respondent] is not looking for work?" Responses were classified as one or more of the following:

—Believes no work is available in his or her line of work or area;

—Couldn't find any work;

—Lacks necessary schooling, training, skills, or experience;

—Believes employers think that the respondent is too young or too old;

—Has other personal handicap in finding a job;

—Can't arrange child care;

—Has family responsibilities;

—Is in school or other training;

—Suffers from ill health or physical disability;

—Other;

—Doesn't know.

If respondents participating in the CPS indicate that they believe no work is available, cannot find work, lack necessary schooling, think employers find them too young or too old, or have some personal handicap (e.g., racial discrimination or a criminal record), or if they were eligible for the military draft (in past years), then they are classified as discouraged workers. If, on the other hand, they give reasons such as an inability to arrange child care, family responsibilities, enrollment in school, ill health, or physical disability, then they are excluded from the discouraged category. In those cases where respondents select reasons from *both* categories, they are *not* considered to be discouraged.[4]

Although the BLS includes discouraged workers in the working-age population (i.e., people who are 16 years of age and older), they do not consider them to be part of the labor force, which as previously noted includes only the employed and unemployed. The employed are those who have been working for pay, while the unemployed are those who are not only jobless but also actively looking for work. All others not in these two groups, including discouraged workers, are "not in the labor force." Precise labor-force definitions used in the CPS are provided in Table 2.1.

These definitional conventions exclude discouraged workers from the nation's unemployed because they are not considered to be part of the labor force nor to be unemployed. Excluding them has the effect of lowering both the total number considered to be unemployed and the reported unemployment percentage.

Another limitation of the BLS reporting program is that information about discouraged workers is published only quarterly for a subsample of households and is not available at the state or local levels. Excessive cost and time constraints on interviewing are offered as reasons for these omissions (see Finegan 1978).

Existing Knowledge Base

Labor economists working with BLS data have focused most of their attention on the following questions:

1. How many discouraged workers are there? Has the size of this group, compared with others in the working-age population, changed over time?

2. How do the demographic characteristics of discouraged workers compare with those of other labor-force groups, especially the unemployed?

3. Why are some people discouraged about finding a job?

Table 2.1
CPS Labor-Force Definitions

```
******************************************************************
Employed Workers   In  order  to  be  considered  employed,  a  person
must have been engaged in one of the  following activities during
the week prior to the interview:

     1.  Worked any time at all as a paid employee
     2.  Any self-employed work
     3.  Any work on their own farm
     4.  Worked 15 hours or more at unpaid farm work
     5.  Worked 15 hours or more unpaid at a family business
     6.  Not working, but temporarily absent because of: (a)
         illness, (b) vacation, (c) bad weather, (d) labor
         dispute, (e) time off for personal reasons

Unemployed Workers   To  be  considered  unemployed,  a  person must
not have worked during the week prior to  the interview  and must
have been available for work as follows:

     1.  Engaged in job-seeking activity in the past four weeks
     2.  Waiting to be called back from a layoff
     3.  Waiting to start a new job in thirty days

Not in the Labor  Force   All other  persons 16 years of age and
over not engaged or employed as above and not in the armed forces
are classified as not in the labor force.  Includes:

     1.  Discouraged workers
     2.  Ill and disabled
     3.  Housewives or househusbands
     4.  Retired
     5.  Students

Civilian Labor  Force   The civilian  labor force is comprised of
all civilians who are  either employed or unemployed  according to
the above definitions.  Members of the armed forces are excluded.

******************************************************************

Source:  National Commission on Employment and Unemployment
         Statistics, 1979.
```

4. How has the composition of the discouraged worker population changed over time?

5. How long have discouraged workers been without jobs?

6. How many intend to look for work in the near future?

7. How would official unemployment rates be affected if discouraged workers were included in them (as discussed in chapter 1)? How should the discouraged worker population be treated in calculating other measures of economic hardship (such as income level)?

8. How do changes in the national economy affect the numbers of discouraged workers?

Table 2.2
Civilian Employment, Unemployment, and Persons Not in the Labor Force, by
Activity Status and Reasons: Annual Averages for 1984 (in thousands of persons)

```
****************************************************************

Civilian non-institutional population, aged 16 and over    176,383

Civilian labor force                                       113,544

   Employed                                                105,005
   Unemployed                                                8,539

Not in the labor force                                      62,839

Do not want job now:                                        56,768
   Going to school                                           6,537
   Ill, disabled                                             3,995
   Keeping house                                            28,051
   Retired                                                  13,774
   Other                                                     4,441

Want job now, by reason for not seeking work:                6,070
   School attendance                                         1,544
   Ill health, disability                                      801
   Home responsibilities                                     1,378
   Think cannot get job (discouraged)                        1,283
   All other reasons                                         1,064

****************************************************************

Source:  BLS, Employment and Earnings, January 1985.

Note: The sum of persons in the detailed not-in-the-labor-force
      categories differs slightly from the total shown above
      because of the use of different weights in aggregating
      these data.
```

Answers to these questions constitute most of what has been known until now about discouraged workers.

Scientific knowledge about the discouraged worker has been expertly summarized and expanded by T. Aldrich Finegan in his analysis for the National Commission on Employment and Unemployment Statistics (1978). Work since this seminal publication has sought mostly to extend and update past research rather than to set sights on new targets. Here, the findings reported by Finegan, and those reported in several follow-up studies from the 1980s, have been updated where possible, using data for 1984.

Numbers. Discouraged workers are a relatively small group when compared with the entire working-age population, but are large enough to be of public concern in the debate about unemployment (see Table 2.2). The BLS reported that the annual average number of discouraged workers nationwide in 1984 was approximately 1,283,000. This contrasts with a civilian working-age population of 176,383,000 people, of whom 113,544,000 are considered to be in the labor force. Of those in the labor force, 105,005,000 were employed and 8,539,000 were unemployed.

Discouraged workers thus represent only about 0.7 percent of the civilian working-age population. Converted into proportions of other groups, there are:

—7.3 discouraged workers for every 1,000 people in the working-age population;

—11.3 per 1,000 workers in the labor force;

—12.2 per 1,000 employed workers;

—150.3 per 1,000 unemployed workers; and

—20.4 per 1,000 adults not in the labor force.

The census figures at a single point in time do not capture turnover in the discouraged worker population. Spells of discouragement end when people who are discouraged accept jobs or give up wanting a job. People "fall into" discouragement after being employed or unsuccessfully looking for work or perhaps without ever having looked. Although 1,283,000 people were discouraged at one time in 1984, there were hundreds of thousands more who were discouraged workers *at some time* during the year. In the Survey of Income and Program Participation (SIPP), 1,603,000 individuals experienced some discouragement during the period from January to July 1985.

Discouraged workers were not the largest group outside the labor force wanting, but not seeking, employment. Of 6,070,000 people wanting but not seeking jobs at any one time in 1984, discouraged workers accounted for only 21 percent. Those who reported attending school (1,544,000 or 25 percent) and those with home responsibilities (1,378,000 or 23 percent) slightly outnumbered discouraged workers.

Demographics. Demographics reported by the BLS on a quarterly basis are limited to age, sex, and race. Statistics concerning marital status, education, veteran's status, and ethnicity are gathered by the BLS but not published.

Discouraged workers are a heterogeneous population consisting of several large groups (see Table 2.3), as summarized here:

- Females (62 percent of the discouraged) dominate the discouraged worker population nearly two to one (males comprise 38 percent).

- When age and sex categories are combined, females aged 25 to 59 years (38 percent) constitute the largest discouraged group.

- People under 20 years of age or over 60 years represent one-fourth (27 percent) of the discouraged.

- Minorities (40 percent of the discouraged) are overrepresented in the discouraged worker population relative to their proportion of the working-age population; minority females are even more so (25 percent).

Table 2.3

Discouraged and Unemployed Workers by Age, Sex, and Race in 1984 (as percentages)

```
*******************************************************************
Demographic:                               Discouraged    Unemployed
------------------------------------------------------------------


Males, 16 and Over                            38.1          55.6
   16-19                                        6.4           9.5
   20-24                                        8.1          12.0
   25-59                                       17.0          29.3
   60+                                          6.6           2.3

Females, 16 and Over                          62.9          44.4
   16-19                                        5.8           8.0
   20-24                                       10.2           9.5
   25-59                                       38.0          25.5
   60+                                          8.0           1.4

White males, 16 and Over                      24.8          42.2

Black and Other Males, 16 and Over            14.8          11.7

White Females, 16 and Over                    39.4          32.5

Black and Other Females, 16 and Over          24.8          10.7

All Persons, 16 and Over (in
   thousands)                                1,283         8,539

*******************************************************************
```

Source: BLS, Employment and Earnings, January 1985, Annual
          Average.

- White males (25 percent) outnumber minority males (15 percent), but by a much smaller ratio than in the whole population.

Not only are the officially discouraged a diverse group, but also they differ, on average, from the officially unemployed. Compared with discouraged workers, the unemployed:

—are more likely to be males (56 percent of the unemployed versus 38 percent of the discouraged);

—have about equal proportions of males (29 percent) and females (26 percent) in the age group between 25 and 59 years, rather than a predominance of females (38 percent) over males (17 percent);

—are somewhat more likely to be white (75 percent versus 64 percent); and

—are much less likely to be minority females (11 percent versus 25 percent).

Table 2.4
Reasons for Discouragement in 1984 (in thousands)

```
*****************************************************************
Reasons:                                      N            %
-----------------------------------------------------------------


Job Market Factors                           919         71.6
   Believes no work available                373         29.1
   Could not find a job                       546         42.6

Personal Factors                             364         28.4
   Lacks schooling or skills                 143         11.1
   Employers think too young or
      too old                                132         10.3
   Other personal handicap                    89          6.9

Total                                      1,283        100.0

*****************************************************************

Source:   BLS, Employment and Earnings, January 1985.
```

In other words, the unemployed are demographically more like the employed population than are the discouraged.

Reasons for Discouragement. The BLS assigns workers to one of two categories of reasons for discouragement: job-market factors (those who believe no work is available or that they cannot find work) or personal factors (those who say they lack necessary schooling or face discrimination due to employers' perceptions of age or another personal handicap) (Flaim 1973).

Based on survey responses (see Table 2.4), nearly three out of four discouraged workers, or about 919,000 people in 1984, were not seeking work either because they believed that no work was available (29 percent) or because they could not find work when they had looked in the past (43 percent). The personal reasons given for not looking for a job, although much less frequently cited (28 percent), suggest that about 364,000 people believe they have some deficiency or handicap preventing them from landing jobs. Lack of schooling or job skills is the most common concern (11 percent), age discrimination (being either too young or too old) is the next (10 percent), and only 7 percent report some personal barrier related to other forms of discrimination or handicap.

Duration. People who have never held a job or have been absent from the labor force for a long period of time may differ in important ways from other discouraged workers. Those who haven't worked in a long time may also be even more dissimilar than other discouraged workers to the unemployed, who as a group tend to have been jobless for shorter periods. The BLS provides one measure of work experience by asking how long it has been since a person last worked.

Using data from a special survey of discouraged workers in 1983, Flaim (1984) distinguished discouraged workers from the unemployed on the basis of their

Table 2.5
Discouraged Worker Employment History for Period 1979–83 (as percentages)

```
*****************************************************************
                                    Y   E   A   R
When Last Worked:       1979    1980        1981    1982    1983
-----------------------------------------------------------------
Never worked            13.2    15.6        12.8    14.2    14.0

Last worked more than
  5 years ago           20.6    21.9        20.0    21.6    20.2

Last worked 1 to 5
  years ago             32.8    29.0        33.2    34.2    38.0

Worked last year        33.3    33.6        34.0    30.0    27.7

Total (000's)            766     993       1,103   1,567   1,641

*****************************************************************
```

Source: Flaim (1984, p. 9).

separation in time from employment (see also Finegan 1978) (see Table 2.5). He notes that:

—about four-fifths of the discouraged worker population had worked at some time during their adult lives; and

—nearly one-third had worked within the last year; *but*

—more than one-half had been out of work longer than one year.

Flaim did not examine demographic differences in his analysis, but in a similar study in 1977, Finegan (1978) reported differences for age and sex:

—male discouraged workers were more likely to have recently worked than females (although males and females who had never worked were found in the same proportions);

—males in the prime working-age groups (20 to 59 years) and females aged 20 to 24 were much more likely than others to have recently worked; and

—older workers (over 59 years) were likely to have been out of the labor force much longer than others but were more likely than others to have worked at some time.

These findings reflect the general domination of employment, until recently, by prime working-age males.

Reason for Unemployment. The BLS has attempted to determine how economic conditions increase or decrease the discouraged worker population (see

Table 2.6
Reasons for Leaving Last Job for Those Who Worked in Previous 12 Months, 1979–83 (as percentages)

```
**************************************************************
                                          Y   E   A   R
Reason For Leaving Last Job:    1979   1980   1981   1982   1983
----------------------------------------------------------------
```

Reason For Leaving Last Job:	1979	1980	1981	1982	1983
School, family	15.6	16.2	16.8	13.2	12.5
Health	6.3	3.9	4.0	2.6	2.2
Retirement	3.1	2.4	2.9	3.6	3.5
Economic problems	48.8	53.9	54.0	57.3	61.7
Other reasons	26.2	24.6	22.1	23.3	20.2
Total (000's)	256	334	374	468	455

```
**************************************************************
```

Source: Flaim (1984, p. 9).

Flaim 1984). In their special studies in 1979 and 1983, BLS researchers concluded that "only" about one-half of those leaving jobs in the past year had done so for economic reasons (see Table 2.6). This understates the importance of economic factors, which were cited more often than any others. As the economy deteriorates, job leavers are increasingly likely to report economic reasons: 48.8 percent in 1979 and rising to 61.7 percent in 1983, a recession year. Published data do not report reasons for leaving a job for those who were jobless more than one year, making it impossible to assess the effects of economic cycles on worker behavior in the labor market. Consequently, the extent of impact of economic cycles on discouraged workers has not yet been adequately explored.

Income. Some people do not work because they do not need to, although they might if offered high enough earnings. Others are readier to work, but cannot find a job. Knowing the household income levels of discouraged workers would indicate who needed and did not need to work.

To our knowledge, BLS data have not been studied to assess the relationship between discouragement and household income. Previous studies relating income to employment status have focused on the unemployed, the working poor, and involuntary part-time workers, but *not* the discouraged worker (see Vietorisz et al. 1975; Gilroy 1975; Miller 1973; Levitan and Taggart 1973). Discouraged worker incomes are not fully reported, although the literature implies that discouraged workers generally have low incomes. How low relative to others has yet to be estimated, and income distinctions within the category of discouraged worker similarly have yet to be made.

Future Intentions. If discouraged workers are serious about entering the labor

Table 2.7
Discouraged Workers by Intent to Look for Work in Next 12 Months by Age and Sex for 1977

```
*****************************************************************
                                 Number      Percent Who Intend
Demographic:                (in thousands)   To Look for Work
-----------------------------------------------------------------

Total, 16 and Over               1,010             78.2

Males, 16 and Over                 317             81.1
   16-19                             69             91.3
   20-24                             47             91.5
   25-59                             94             84.0
   60+                              106             66.0

Females, 16 and Over               694             76.0
   16-19                             90             87.8
   20-24                             91             89.0
   25-59                            405             79.0
   60+                              108             48.1

*****************************************************************
```

Source: Finegan (1978, p. 17).

force, then they should intend to look for work in the near future (e.g., within the next 12 months), at which time, they would officially join the ranks of the unemployed. Once again, using published BLS data for 1977, Finegan (1978) found the following (see Table 2.7)[5]:

— about three-fourths (78 percent) of the discouraged worker population said they intended to look for work within the next 12 months;

— males (78 percent) were no more likely than females (76 percent) to intend to look for work; and

— younger workers, both males and females, were more likely to intend to look for work than were older workers.

Job Search and Employment Success. Discouraged workers interviewed as part of the 1976 and 1983 CPS samples were asked (in separate studies) one year later about their employment experience (Job 1979; Flaim 1984). Nearly one-half had entered the labor force, being either employed or searching for work. Of those who had entered the labor force, one-third remained jobless and one-fourth were employed for some period but eventually left or lost their jobs; two-fifths of those entering the labor force were employed when recontacted. Moreover, more than one-half had made no effort to find a job in the past year. Only 10 percent of all discouraged workers were actually working at the follow-up interview one year after the 1976 interview, and 20 percent were in a job when recontacted one year after the 1983 interview.

To Flaim, the evidence regarding job search and future intentions suggests that "many of the discouraged, although expressing a desire for a job and their intention to look for one, find it very difficult to translate their sentiments into concrete and productive job-seeking efforts" (Flaim 1984, p. 10). That analysis strongly challenges the conventional view of discouragement.

Socioeconomic Change. The number of discouraged workers could be expected to rise gradually as the nation's population increases and to vary over time as the composition of the working-age population changes and with fluctuations in the level of economic activity (Tannewald 1984).

The last two decades have also seen an acceleration of changes in the fundamental structure of the U.S. economy. In the last two decades, many so-called "core" workers have been displaced from seemingly secure jobs in wave after wave of plant closings. Also, during this time, many women who previously would not have considered working outside the home have joined a swelling labor force that now includes a record-high proportion of U.S. adults. The number of jobs requiring either advanced technical or managerial skills, on the one hand, or only basic skills, on the other hand, has increased rapidly, while traditionally high-paying "skilled labor" employment has contracted as a proportion of the total. How do such changes in the structure of the labor force affect the position of discouraged workers?

The number of discouraged workers nearly doubled between 1968, when there were 667,000, and 1984, when there were 1,283,000 (see Table 2.8). During this same period, the working-age population and the labor force both increased by about one-third; so did unemployment rates, while fluctuating from year to year. Thus, the pool of discouraged workers more than doubled (from 3.5 percent to 7.4 percent) rapidly, which helps to account for the emerging interest in them as an object of public policy (U.S. Congress 1986b).

Changes in the demographic composition of discouraged workers also may have contributed to this increased interest and concern (see Table 2.9):

- The proportion of the discouraged who are minority males nearly doubled from 1968 to 1984.

- Minority females became a higher percentage of the discouraged.

- White females declined as a proportion from a majority (53 percent) to less than 40 percent of the discouraged, over the same period.

The parts of the adult population that have made the least economic progress over the last two decades have become a higher proportion of the discouraged, while the group (white females) that has moved most rapidly and easily into the employment mainstream has become a smaller proportion of the discouraged.

Economic Fluctuations. How do economic cycles affect the number of discouraged workers (Ondeck 1978; Flaim 1973; Finegan 1978)? Are they more or less affected by alternative growth and recession than other groups outside

Table 2.8

Reasons for Discouragement: Annual Averages for 1968 to 1984 (as percentages)

****

			Y E A R		
Reason:	1968	1972	1976	1980	1984
Job Market	55.6	70.6	70.6	66.8	71.6
No work available	31.5	31.4	30.3	29.0	29.1
Could not find job	24.1	39.2	40.3	37.8	42.6
Personal	44.5	29.4	29.3	33.2	28.4
Lacks schooling or skills	11.1	10.2	8.6	11.4	11.1
Employers think too old or young	25.6	14.5	16.0	13.7	10.3
Other personal handicap	7.8	4.8	4.7	8.0	6.9
Total (in thousands)	100.0	100.0	100.0	100.0	100.0
	(667)	(765)	(910)	(970)	(1,283)

****

Source: BLS, **Employment and Earnings,** January 1969, 1973, 1977,
1981, 1985, Annual Average.

the labor force who also want jobs? How is the civilian labor force changed by the entry and withdrawal of discouraged workers?

Between 1967 and 1977, the number of discouraged workers varied inversely with the level of economic activity: a one percentage point increase (decrease) in the overall unemployment rate added (subtracted) 115,000 to the total of discouraged workers. However, the pattern differs depending on the reasons given for not looking for work. The numbers of those discouraged for personal reasons (such as schooling or age) did not vary in response to fluctuations in the economy. The number of those discouraged for job-market reasons (such as being unable to find work) did.

Thus, the correlation between numbers of discouraged workers and economic change is not perfect. Rosenblum (1974) was able to improve the correlation between the two indicators by reassigning those people who were discouraged because of age (too young or too old) to the job market (believe no work available or could not find work) category of discouragement. He reasoned that:

> During periods of high-level economic activity, employers, finding labor scarcer, become more flexible. Age limits are the first to be relaxed, and both younger and older workers are employed in greater numbers. On the other side, in recession periods, employers can tighten their age requirements and those outside the prime working years find it harder to obtain employment (1974, p. 28).

Table 2.9

Discouraged Workers by Age, Sex, and Race: Annual Averages for 1968 to 1984 (as percentages)

```
*****************************************************************
                                    Y   E   A   R
Demographic Categories:    1968    1972    1976    1980    1984
-----------------------------------------------------------------
```

Demographic Categories:	1968	1972	1976	1980	1984
Males, 16+	31.9	31.4	35.3	36.2	38.1
16-19	6.3	8.5	7.5	8.9	6.4
20-24	1.5	4.4	4.9	5.7	8.1
25-59	7.9	8.8	11.9	12.0	17.0
60+	16.0	9.8	11.0	9.6	6.6
Females, 16+	68.2	66.8	64.8	63.8	61.9
16-19	10.0	8.9	8.0	8.9	5.8
20-24	7.0	10.5	8.2	9.6	10.2
25-59	36.0	39.2	38.0	36.9	38.0
60+	15.1	10.3	10.4	8.6	8.0
White males, 16+	24.9	24.4	25.5	24.5	24.8
Black and Other Minority Males, 16+	7.0	6.9	9.8	11.5	14.8
White Females, 16+	53.5	51.1	49.6	43.8	39.4
Black and Other Minority Females, 16+	14.7	17.6	15.2	20.1	24.8
Total discouraged	100.0	100.0	100.0	100.0	100.0
(in thousands)	(667)	(765)	(910)	(970)	(1,283)

```
*****************************************************************
```

Source: BLS, Employment and Earnings, January 1968, 1972, 1976, 1980, 1984, Annual Averages.

Deep, long-term structural transformation in the U.S. population and industrial base, overlain by the erratic movements of the business cycle may have made the discouraged worker population less homogeneous (with respect to age, sex, race, and occupation) than was once believed. With continuing rapid transformation of the U.S. economy and population, it is likely also that the discouraged worker population will continue to evolve. Discouraged workers, then, are moving targets for public policy.

Toward Complexity

It is not surprising that knowledge about discouraged workers is fragmentary and incomplete, given the limitations and features of the BLS statistical program and the absence of other data (see Finegan 1978). However, even with the limited information available, it has become more and more obvious that the most common stereotype of the discouraged worker is too simplified to be very useful for policy development.

If the typical discouraged worker fit the stereotype of someone who was first laid off and later gave up looking for work, then discouraged workers might closely resemble the (officially) unemployed; yet the unemployed and discouraged appear to differ in several important ways. Demographically (i.e., by sex, age, and race), discouraged workers include greater proportions of women and older and younger people than the unemployed. Minorities are overrepresented—a trend that is continuing at an increasing rate. In regard to possible degree of attachment to the labor force, as reflected by work history, the discouraged are more likely than the unemployed to have never worked and, if they once worked, to have been out of work for a longer period of time. Many have not bothered to look for work recently and seem only mildly interested in working. It is possible, however, that discouraged workers do not resemble the officially unemployed because the discouraged are only a subset of those unemployed who are least employable. In other words, some evidence suggests that discouraged workers may be the residual of those unemployed who are least competitive in the job market.[6] Even if the latter argument is true, the evidence suggests that the traditional view of discouragement is oversimplified.

SUMMARY

If discouraged workers do not represent an army of workers who have recently dropped out of the labor force, then who are they? Broadly speaking, either they represent people who can and would work if offered a job; or they are people who do not really want to work, would only accept jobs under the most restrictive conditions, or possibly could not work if offered a job. Previous research has not sorted out these possibilities, but it does suggest that discouraged workers are a more heterogeneous population than generally supposed. If they are not like the unemployed, or the employed for that matter, discouraged workers may resemble others who want jobs but who will only consider working on their own terms.

Also in doubt is the extent to which discouraged workers represent a loss of potentially productive human capital. Because many discouraged workers have worked, they do constitute a pool of potential labor. Yet since most have not recently worked, many presumably lack skills and experience, and may have major handicaps that would reduce their potential contribution. Only a closer look at the discouraged workers, their motivations, and their abilities as workers can settle the question of their usefulness in the labor force.

Finally, a revised picture of the discouraged worker would have important implications for public policy. To the extent that this group, like others on the margin of the labor force, represents a loss of productive labor, new forms of assistance or incentives can be used to overcome obstacles or resistance to their participation in work.

NOTES

1. Precise definitions of these concepts are offered by Mincer (1973) and Gastwirth (1973).

2. These numbers are from: Domestic Policy Council on Low Income Opportunity, *Up From Dependency—A Report to the President* (Washington, D.C.: Domestic Policy Council, 1986).

3. As an example, see descriptions and evaluations of the guaranteed income maintenance experiments initiated in the 1960s and 1970s (Munnell 1987).

4. Another 7.4 percent (136,613 individuals) selected two responses. Only one percent (19,026 persons) chose three or more.

5. See also Flaim (1984, p. 9).

6. This has yet to be tested directly with the BLS data, but indirect evidence is often cited using findings on the expressed intentions of discouraged workers to search for work (Flaim 1984). Only two-fifths of those questioned in 1978 had looked for work at any time during the previous year, and only one-third did so in the last three months. This suggests that, on average, discouraged workers are less strongly attached to the labor force than the officially unemployed.

PART II
TOWARD A NEW
PERSPECTIVE

3

PATHS TO DISCOURAGEMENT

The fact that researchers obtain evidence almost exclusively from the monthly Bureau of Labor Statistics (BLS) Current Population Survey and related national surveys may explain why the discouraged worker debate remains unresolved. The BLS gathers and reports only very elementary demographic statistics, while leaving many basic questions unanswered.[1] This appears to have fueled, rather than quelled, speculation about who the discouraged worker really is.

The 1984 special plant-closing supplement to the Current Population Survey (CPS) goes a long way toward putting existing BLS analyses in context and providing a much more differentiated picture of the discouraged worker. Since this data set has only recently become available, it has not yet been fully exploited by labor-market analysts.

This chapter looks at how people come to be discouraged workers. Some of the ambiguity in the discouraged worker debate is cleared away by examining the 1984 CPS and its supplement, which are augmented where possible with survey data from the Youngstown, Ohio, labor-market and plant-closing studies.

The chapter is organized in three parts. An initial section sorts discouraged workers into three groups: (1) "displaced workers," or those who have been laid off either in a plant closing or mass layoff; (2) "other job losers," or those who have lost or quit jobs for reasons other than a plant closing or similar event; and (3) "never worked," or those who have no work experience (refer to Figure 3.1 for precise definitions).[2] Since the CPS plant-closing supplement provides more information about the first of the three groups than about the others, much of the chapter focuses on the discouraged who are also displaced.

When surveyed, displaced workers who were classified as discouraged are

Figure 3.1
A Discouraged Worker Typology

* *

Category	Definition
Displaced	All discouraged workers responding affirmative to the question: "In the past five years, that is, since January 1979 has [respondent] lost or left a job because of a plant closing, an employer going out of business, a layoff from which [respondent] was not recalled, or other similar reasons?" (CPS Supplement).
Other Job Losers	All discouraged workers who have been employed, left a job because of: "personal, family or school; health; retirement or old age; seasonal job completed; slack work or business conditions; temporary non-seasonal job completed, unsatisfactory work arrangements, or other reasons" (Monthly CPS) and responded negatively to the plant closing question (CPS Supplement).
Never Worked	All discouraged workers responding "never worked" to the question: "When did [respondent] last work for pay at a regular job or business, either full- or part-time?" (Monthly CPS).

* *

Note: All three categories of discouragement are mutually exclusive and exhaustive of the discouraged worker population.

compared first with displaced workers who were reemployed (''the rehired'') and second with those who remained unemployed. Next, discouraged workers who left jobs for ''other reasons'' and those who have never worked are analyzed, partly to establish how large each of the three discouraged worker groups is relative to the others. Are most discouraged workers members of the core labor force who have been left out in the cold by a plant closing? Or, are they primarily less experienced or inexperienced workers who are only weakly attached to the labor force?

In a second section, analysis focuses on the first of the three groups of discouraged workers: those involved in plant closings. What kinds of jobs did they hold? What are their demographics? How similar are they to unemployed and rehired workers who were also displaced? Also, discouraged workers displaced by plant closings are compared with discouraged workers whose jobs ended for reasons other than a closing. Are discouraged workers more likely to have lost jobs in a closing or for other reasons? How do the two groups of discouraged workers differ demographically? How do discouraged and unemployed workers who were not laid off in a closing differ?

In this chapter's last section, the two categories of discouraged workers *with* work experience—those who were either involved in a closing or left jobs for other reasons—are contrasted to the third category of discouraged workers: those *without* work experience. How similar or different are the three groups? In the chapter summary, the implications of this analysis for the discouraged worker debate are further elaborated.

THREE TYPES OF DISCOURAGEMENT: DISPLACED, OTHER JOB LOSERS, NEVER WORKED

The most direct way to ascertain whether or not workers have been laid off in a plant closing through no fault of their own is to ask them in so many words. The 1984 plant-closing supplement was the first national survey to ask workers this question. Until now, therefore, analysts have relied on self-reports about why people left jobs and how long it has been since they worked. Thus, it could not be determined how many discouraged workers were displaced workers down on their luck, how many were people who had quit working voluntarily, and how many had never worked nor seriously looked for work.

The 1984 supplement settles part of the argument. Discouraged workers, contrary to the conventional view, are only rarely people who had worked steadily all of their lives but, through no fault of their own, were laid off in a plant closing. In the five-year period from 1979 to 1984, nearly 12 million workers lost jobs due to plant closings or major work-force reductions.[3] Of these, only 0.5 percent, or 61,000 workers, were discouraged as of January 1984. If discouraged workers had been considered officially unemployed, just 1.7 percent of the jobless would have been classified as discouraged. Thus, discouraged workers are an even smaller proportion of the displaced worker population than they are of all unemployed persons. *This single statistical comparison demonstrates beyond a doubt that the conventional interpretation of discouragement is inaccurate.*

What proportion of discouraged workers do fit the conventional stereotype, that is, are victims of massive layoffs or plant closings? Of more than 400,000 discouraged workers identified in the January 1984 CPS, only 15 percent were identified in the plant-closing supplement as being involved in a plant closing or mass layoff in the preceding five years.[4]

In Youngstown—a metropolitan area that experienced a series of massive

Table 3.1

Year in which Discouraged and Unemployed Workers Were Laid Off in Plant Closings from 1979–84 (as percentages)

```
*********************************************************************
```

Reason:	Plant Closing*	All Job Losses*
Personal, family, or school	5.0	25.4
Health	0.0	13.1
Retirement or old age	1.9	2.4
Seasonal job completed	12.1	11.2
Slack work	49.3	16.8
Temporary non-seasonal job completed	10.8	4.2
Unsatisfactory work conditions	1.8	14.0
Other	19.1	12.9
N	61,243	163,719

```
*********************************************************************
```

Source: 1984 CPS and Plant Closing Supplement.

*See Footnote 2 for definitions.

layoffs between 1978 and 1984, which affected 20,000 steelworkers alone (Buss and Redburn 1983)—in roughly the same period, 17 percent (between 800 and 900 people) of the discouraged worker population had been laid off in a closing. Even in Youngstown, displaced workers do not predominate among discouraged workers.

The group of displaced workers who were classified as discouraged when interviewed is about two-thirds the size of the group of discouraged workers who have no work experience. Those without work experience numbered a little less than 100,000 and constituted 24 percent of the discouraged workers interviewed. The third group of discouraged workers—*people who lost or quit jobs for reasons other than a plant closing or layoff*—then, *constitute the lion's share of discouraged workers*, about 250,000 people or 60 percent of the discouraged workers sampled in 1984.

Why is the displaced discouraged worker population so small? Discouragement, for most displaced workers, is probably short-term. Looking back from 1984 at the layoff of those who became discouraged workers (see Table 3.1), most of the unemployed (those actively searching for work) had been laid off relatively recently—within the last two years. More and more workers are ab-

Table 3.2
Discouraged Workers Involved and Not Involved in Plant Closings by Original Reason for Leaving Job (as percentages)

```
*********************************************************************
        Year:      Discouraged     Unemployed      Rehired
--------------------------------------------------------------------

        1979         10.5            5.3            11.8
        1980          7.5            7.3            16.8
        1981         30.2           12.1            21.7
        1982         34.5           22.9            27.0
        1983         17.4           50.2            21.5
        1984          0.4            2.1             1.1

*********************************************************************

Source:   1984 CPS and Plant Closing Supplement.
```

sorbed into the labor force as time passes. Most soon recover and go back to work. A small group become discouraged, but in most cases, only after a period of active job search. In fact, fewer than 20 percent of those who were discouraged in January 1984 had been laid off as recently as 1983.

Analysis of discouragement among steelworkers laid off in the Youngstown Sheet and Tube plant closing of 1977 shows a similar pattern. One year after the closing, 58 percent of the unemployed reported discouragement about finding a job. As of 1985, nearly a decade later, only 2 percent were discouraged. Thus, if many displaced workers pass through a brief period of discouragement, most are eventually reemployed. A "snapshot" of workers laid off in a five-year period understates the proportion who have been discouraged at one time during the transition to new jobs.

All displaced workers interviewed in the 1984 CPS supplement were asked to indicate why they had lost or left their last jobs (see chapter 2). It is important to note that the last job held may be either the one from which the worker was displaced or a job acquired subsequent to displacement. Of the 61,000 displaced workers identified by the 1984 CPS and its supplement, 28 percent, or about 17,000 workers, reported leaving their most recent jobs for reasons not related to a closing or layoff. These reasons include the following: personal, family, or school (5 percent); retirement or old age (2 percent); unsatisfactory work conditions (2 percent); and other reasons (19 percent) (see Table 3.2). Of the remaining 72 percent, 12 percent had most recently been employed in seasonal jobs, and another 11 percent had been only temporarily employed. About 30,000 workers reported "slack work" as the reason for job loss, suggesting either that they had not worked since their initial displacement or had been displaced from two or more jobs in succession. The diverse reasons given for leaving a last job suggest a pattern that is not measured directly by the survey, that many of those laid off quickly find other work but not necessarily stable or desirable employment. Periods of discouragement may occur before, between, and after those periods of temporary reemployment.

The remarkable capacity of the U.S. economy to reabsorb displaced workers during this period of industrial restructuring helps explain why more workers were not discouraged when interviewed (Flaim and Seghal 1985). Of the more than 5.1 million workers with at least three years on the job who were displaced from 1979 to 1984, 3.1 million (60 percent) were working as of January 1984. Another 1.3 million (26 percent) were unemployed but had not given up looking for work. Only 700,000 (14 percent) had left the labor force.

In the depressed Youngstown labor market, the layoff impacts were somewhat more severe. Some 45 percent of displaced workers were reemployed within five years, while 35 percent were unemployed but searching for work. Twenty percent had left the labor force, often through early retirement. Nationally, for most displaced workers who experience discouragement, unemployment is fortunately a transitory experience. In a depressed market, the majority may remain out of the labor force for a long time. Yet, even here, the conventional view of discouragement as the reaction to an unsuccessful job search following a layoff does not describe the experience of most of those classified as discouraged.

PLANT CLOSINGS AND DISCOURAGEMENT

Why do some displaced workers become and remain discouraged, while others, although unemployed, continue to look for work? Why are most displaced workers able to find replacement jobs, while others remain unemployed or become discouraged? Answers to these questions are suggested by comparing the groups' demographics and work experience.

Demographics

Demographic characteristics are consistently correlated with labor-force participation. Those having difficulty entering or remaining in the labor force include the very old and very young, members of racial or ethnic minority groups that have experienced discrimination, women with traditional child-care responsibilities, and those lacking education or job skills (Levitan et al. 1981). Older (60 years or more) or younger (19 years or less) workers both may have problems participating: older workers may be perceived to be past their prime or may have disabilities, while younger ones have yet to acquire exprience or skills necessary to be competitive. Minorities often have difficulty, both because of past and present discrimination and because they lack skills or experience, having been excluded from full social participation in the past. Women, especially in seeking jobs traditionally dominated by men, may be less competitive because of discrimination or past exclusion. Married people, especially women who have child-care responsibilities, may have difficulty finding enough time for work. Finally, because education is often required as a basis for acquiring specialized job skills,

Table 3.3

Demographics of Discouraged, Unemployed, and Rehired Workers Laid Off in Plant Closings (as percentages)

****

Demographic Category:	Discouraged	Unemployed	Rehired
Education			
elementary	13.6	8.8	4.6
some high school	24.7	18.1	10.7
high school	49.3	47.5	43.5
some college	5.2	17.1	23.4
college	1.1	5.8	10.7
post grad	6.3	2.6	7.1
Race			
white	69.7	77.5	89.7
black	26.9	19.8	8.3
other	3.3	2.7	2.0
Sex			
male	42.8	65.9	66.0
female	57.2	34.1	34.0
Age			
19	NA	NA	NA
20-24	16.8	18.7	18.0
25-59	74.4	76.2	79.9
60+	8.8	5.2	3.0
Marital Status			
married	56.0	60.7	64.9
single	23.2	13.6	23.6
others	20.8	25.7	11.2

****

Source: 1984 CPS and Plant Closing Supplement.

the uneducated generally are less employable than the educated. Even when employment is available to these groups, the range of attractive job opportunities open to them may be very narrow.

Among displaced workers, the discouraged differ significantly from the unemployed and the reemployed (as of January 1984) in terms of several demographic dimensions. Education, race, sex, and marital status account for most of the differences, while age comparisons reveal no differences (see Table 3.3). Displaced discouraged workers are much less educated than either the unemployed or rehired. Discouraged workers are more than two times (38 percent) more likely than the rehired (15 percent) to have dropped out of school before obtaining a high school diploma and somewhat more likely to have dropped out than the unemployed (27 percent). In contrast, rehired workers are three times (41 percent) more likely than the discouraged (13 percent) to have gone to college.

Table 3.4

Length of Time Employed before a Plant Closing by Discouraged, Unemployed, and Rehired Workers (as percentages)

****

Length of time: (years)	Discouraged	Unemployed	Rehired
0	16.1	25.6	21.5
1	21.9	15.5	17.7
2	32.0	14.1	17.3
3	3.6	9.1	11.4
4	2.2	5.9	6.0
5	0.0	5.4	6.2
6-10	10.9	12.3	11.6
11-15	1.4	5.6	4.1
16-20	6.4	3.3	2.8
21-25	2.0	1.4	0.9
26-30	0.0	1.3	0.7
30+	3.4	0.7	0.3
Total	100.0	100.0	100.0

****

Source: 1984 CPS and Plant Closing Supplement.

Unemployed workers are twice (26 percent) as likely as the discouraged to have attended college.

Displaced discouraged workers are three times (30 percent) more likely to be a minority group member than are the rehired (10 percent). Nearly two-thirds (57 percent) of the discouraged but only one-third (34 percent) of the rehired and unemployed are women.

All of these differences suggest that those who remain discouraged months or years after being laid off are a residual group who face social or personal barriers to reemployment.

Job Tenure

The length of tenure of employment prior to layoff also may be a clue to prospects for reemployment following layoffs due to a closing or retrenchment. Workers with less experience may be the last rehired, as well as the first fired, in a surplus labor market. This seems to be especially true for women, minorities, the young, and to some extent, the old and the less educated.

The evidence does not appear to support these hypotheses, however. Whether subsequently discouraged, unemployed, or rehired, displaced workers had nearly identical patterns of job tenure prior to layoff: three-fourths of each group had held a job five years or less before being laid off (see Table 3.4). A comparison of job tenure, then, suggests that the subsequent employment status of a displaced worker does not tell us anything about his or her degree of attachment to the labor force.[5]

Table 3.5
Average Weekly Earnings for Discouraged, Unemployed, and Rehired Workers Laid Off in Plant Closings (as percentages)

****

Weekly Income: (dollars)	Discouraged	Unemployed	Rehired
0–100	21.3	9.5	8.4
101–200	31.8	34.1	31.2
201–300	18.3	22.2	24.7
301–400	16.5	15.9	16.8
401–500	3.3	9.6	9.1
501–600	2.2	3.7	4.1
601–700	5.8	2.7	2.3
701–800	0.0	0.8	1.5
801–900	0.0	0.3	0.6
900+	0.7	1.1	1.3
Totals	100.0	100.0	100.0
N	53,055	3,154,082	7,432,231

****

Source: 1984 CPS and Plant Closing Supplement.

Average Earnings

Wages measure the value of a worker in the marketplace. Those with higher earnings prior to displacement probably have higher-level or broader skills and experience. Following a shutdown, expectations are, *ceteris paribus*, that the higher-wage earner is more employable.

When they were working, displaced discouraged workers on the whole earned somewhat less than either their still unemployed or their subsequently rehired counterparts (see Table 3.5). Discouraged workers were twice as likely to have earned $100 or less a week than the unemployed or rehired.[6] However, as one moves up the weekly earnings scale, disparities between the groups begin to disappear; 71 percent of the discouraged, 66 percent of the unemployed, and 64 percent of the rehired had earned less than $300 weekly.[7]

Displaced discouraged workers fared less well than others in wages because they tended to hold part-time jobs and had lower-level skills, as will be shown in upcoming sections.

Sectoral Employment

As already noted, the industrial base of the nation has been in rapid transition for the last decade. Obsolete uncompetitive facilities and firms have given way to new foreign and domestic competitors; in the 1982–83 period, a deep recession compounded the dislocations produced by structural change. Different industries

Table 3.6
Industrial Sectors from which Discouraged, Unemployed, and Rehired Workers Were Laid Off (as percentages)

```
***********************************************************************
```

Sector:	Discouraged	Unemployed	Rehired
Agriculture	0.4	2.3	2.5
Mining	4.0	3.3	2.5
Construction	7.2	12.8	10.9
Manufacture-Durable	18.4	26.8	25.4
Manufacture-Non-durable	29.9	14.5	14.0
Transport	1.4	5.4	5.4
Communication	2.5	0.2	0.9
Utility	0.6	0.8	0.4
Wholesale	3.1	4.9	5.7
Retail	8.1	11.3	10.8
Finance/Insurance/Real Estate	0.0	1.5	2.8
Private House Service	0.0	0.0	0.0
Business and Repair	0.0	5.8	6.4
Personal Service	7.0	2.1	1.8
Entertainment & Recreation	0.0	1.7	1.5
Hospital	0.5	0.4	0.1
Medical/Exc. Hospital	0.0	0.8	1.7
Educational	0.0	0.4	0.4
Social Service	0.0	1.6	1.2
Other Professional	7.6	1.0	2.8
Forest/Fish	0.0	0.2	0.4
Public Administration	9.3	2.3	2.4
Totals	100.0	100.0	100.0
N	61,000	3,490,602	8,353,299

```
***********************************************************************
```

Source: 1984 CPS and Plant Closing Supplement.

were affected to varying degrees and in different ways by these economic shifts.[8] Manufacturing employment declined overall, while employment in various service sectors grew rapidly. Steel production in the United States was sharply reduced as foreign steel companies made inroads to domestic markets, and overall demand for steel stagnated worldwide. Many other basic industries experienced declines nearly as sharp. Workers in these industries were more likely not only to be laid off, but also to have difficulty finding replacement work in their fields of expertise.

The industries in which most displaced discouraged workers once worked differ from those in which the unemployed and rehired had worked (see Table 3.6). Nearly one-half of the layoffs for all three groups (discouraged, 48 percent; unemployed, 41 percent; and rehired, 39 percent) originated in manufacturing. However, discouraged workers (30 percent) were twice as likely as the unemployed (15 percent) or rehired (14 percent) to be laid off from nondurable goods[9] manufacturing jobs.

Table 3.7
Occupations of Discouraged, Unemployed, and Rehired Workers Laid Off in Plant Closings (as percentages)

****

Occupation:	Discouraged	Unemployed	Rehired
Executive/Admin/Management	1.9	5.6	10.2
Professional Spec	5.6	3.4	7.0
Technician	0.0	1.8	2.9
Sales	11.8	6.8	11.0
Administrative Support	15.7	10.0	10.4
Protective Service	0.9	1.3	0.7
Other Service	8.0	6.9	5.8
Precise Product	14.3	19.4	19.5
Machine Operator	21.5	21.3	17.9
Transportation	4.9	6.3	5.7
Handlers	12.4	14.3	6.5
Farm/Forest/Fish	3.2	2.8	2.3
Totals	100.0	100.0	100.0
N	61,000	3,490,602	8,353,301

****

Source: 1984 CPS and Plant Closing Supplement.

Occupation

Occupational data provide a different picture of the work force than data concerning sectoral employment: occupations tend to cut across industries. An accountant can, for example, find employment in any firm where large amounts of money are managed. By contrast, a steelworker without a craft or transferable skills is confined to employment in a narrow range of firms.

Occupational comparisons reveal some important differences among the three categories of displaced worker (see Table 3.7). Discouraged workers had worked in lower-status jobs than the others. This may have limited their reemployability. Rehired workers, for instance, were two times more likely to have worked in executive or management jobs than were discouraged workers. In contrast, discouraged workers were much more likely than the rehired to have been unskilled material handlers.[10]

Full- or Part-Time Work

Most people who work do so for 40 hours or more each week. However, some people who need full-time jobs to make ends meet can only find part-time work. Others choose part-time work, either because they desire more leisure or because their circumstances constrain the number of hours available for work. Part-time jobs are often seen as less desirable or second-rate, in part because wages are usually low and benefits few.

Table 3.8

Part- and Full-Time Jobs and Demographics for Discouraged, Unemployed, and Rehired Workers Involved in a Plant Closing (as percentages)

****

Demographic Category:	Part-Time			Full-Time		
	Discouraged	Unemployed	Rehired	Discouraged	Unemployed	Rehired
Sex						
male	0.0	39.0	35.4	52.9	70.1	69.5
female	100.0	61.0	64.6	47.1	29.9	30.5
Race						
white	61.1	72.9	89.7	72.0	78.0	90.2
black	38.9	24.9	8.4	23.8	19.4	7.7
other	0.0	2.2	1.9	4.1	2.6	2.2
Age						
20-24	34.9	34.5	35.1	12.3	17.1	15.9
25-59	45.1	61.5	62.0	81.7	77.4	81.0
60+	20.0	4.0	3.0	6.0	5.5	3.0
Marital						
married	48.1	49.7	52.1	58.1	61.3	66.8
single	34.9	12.7	10.6	17.2	25.0	11.3
other	17.0	37.6	37.3	24.5	13.8	22.0
Education						
elementary	17.0	4.8	3.1	12.6	9.5	4.8
some high school	19.9	16.7	6.0	26.3	18.1	11.3
high school	43.3	47.1	40.2	50.2	47.3	43.9
some college	15.7	22.7	25.0	2.5	16.4	23.2
college	3.0	4.9	15.7	0.6	5.9	10.1
post grad	0.0	3.8	10.0	7.7	2.8	6.7

****

Source: 1984 CPS and Plant Closing Supplement.

Discouraged workers were more likely than other displaced workers to have held part-time jobs prior to layoff (see Table 3.8). About one-fifth of the discouraged workers had held part-time jobs, compared with 11 percent of the unemployed and 10 percent of the rehired (not shown in table).

Among the workers losing *part-time* jobs, the unemployed and rehired groups were demographically similar to each other, but very different from the discouraged. Discouraged workers included proportionately more women, blacks, elderly, single, and less-educated persons than the others. These groups have usually been overrepresented in the secondary labor force, as well as among those outside the labor force.

Males dominated those laid off from *full-time* jobs, but were an even higher proportion of those who remained unemployed or were rehired by January 1984 than of those who were then discouraged. Both the unemployed and rehired tended to be more educated than their counterparts among the discouraged.

Table 3.9

Weeks Unemployed Following a Plant Closing for Discouraged, Unemployed, and Rehired Workers (as percentages)

```
**********************************************************************
```

Weeks:	Discouraged	Unemployed	Rehired
0-26	22.9	53.0	72.8
27-52	11.7	17.9	16.8
53-80	18.6	11.8	5.1
81-99	46.8	17.3	5.3
Totals	100.0	100.0	100.0
N	61,168	3,430,864	8,163,444

```
**********************************************************************
```

Source: 1984 CPS and Plant Closing Supplement.

Note: BLS limited responses to 99 weeks.

Weeks without Work

Some evidence suggests that the longer a displaced worker continues to be unemployed, the less likely that worker is to return to employment and the more likely he or she is to drop out of the labor force (Buss and Redburn 1987).

The 1984 survey does not identify workers laid off in more than one closing, since questions only refer to the longest job held. Also, in the CPS plant-closing supplement, all unemployment spells that followed a closing lasting more than 99 weeks are lumped together in one category.[11] Despite these limitations, the evidence shows that the discouraged, unemployed, and rehired differ considerably in the length of time since layoff (see Table 3.9). Most of the displaced and discouraged (65 percent) had been without work for more than one year—a far greater proportion than that for the unemployed (47 percent) and especially the rehired (27 percent). Discouraged workers (85 percent) were much more likely than either the unemployed (52 percent) or the rehired (41 percent) to have exhausted whatever unemployment insurance benefits they had received. The disparity in duration of joblessness is even greater when looking only at the proportions of workers who had been out of work for 26 weeks or less; this corresponds to the period during which most workers receive unemployment insurance. Spells of joblessness lasted less than this period for only 23 percent of those who were identified as discouraged in January 1984, but for 53 percent of the unemployed and 73 percent of the rehired.

In all three groups, blacks were at least twice as likely as whites to have been jobless for two years. Within the discouraged worker category, older and younger workers had longer jobless spells than those of prime working age. These patterns are all consistent with the conventional view of discouragement as a stage of frustration following an unsuccessful search for employment.

PLANT CLOSINGS VERSUS JOB LOSS FOR OTHER REASONS

It is more common for labor-market studies to concern themselves with current labor-force status than with the circumstances of job loss (see Buss 1986b). Thus, analysts tend to treat the unemployed as a single group, without regard for the diverse paths by which people reach a common status. An example of how this can lead to confusion is given here.

Studies have shown that unemployed people are more likely to be child abusers than those who are employed (National Institute of Mental Health 1985). Other work indicates that the incidence of child abuse varies directly with the unemployment rate. But, the incidence of child abuse was low among workers in Youngstown who were displaced due to steel-mill closings in the 1978–82 period (see Buss and Redburn 1987).

What accounts for this phenomenon? The unemployed, generally, are a disparate group, including public assistance recipients, teenage parents, the mentally disabled, school dropouts, as well as those who recently lost well-paying, seemingly secure jobs. Some unemployed have difficulty obtaining work, lose jobs quickly, have little interest in working steadily, and perhaps have little earning power. Some of these people abuse their children. Layoff victims, in contrast, are experienced workers, who rarely become child abusers, despite the stress of being laid off.

If plant closings produce, on average, different kinds of unemployed people than individualized job loss, then displaced workers—either discouraged or officially unemployed—ought to be different from those who lost or gave up jobs for reasons other than a plant closing or layoff. Before the CPS plant-closing supplement became available, comparisons across different kinds of job loss were limited to categories provided in the BLS monthly CPS.[12] This created problems in interpretation. As an example, a worker may report leaving the labor force because of retirement. On the surface, this may appear not to be related in any way to a closing; yet if the retirement was premature and was forced on the worker because of a closing, then the worker is displaced.

The CPS 1984 plant-closing supplement allows for the distinction between job loss due to displacement and job loss for other reasons.[13] Differences between the discouraged displaced and other discouraged job losers are most clearly revealed by a comparison of the two groups' demographics.

Demographics

When displaced discouraged workers are compared with discouraged workers losing jobs for other reasons, the two groups are seen to differ in terms of

Table 3.10
Demographics of Discouraged and Unemployed Workers Laid Off in a Plant Closing and Laid Off for Other Reasons (as percentages)

****

Demographic Category:	Discouraged		Unemployed	
	Plant Closing	Other Job Loss	Plant Closing	Other Job Loss
Education				
elementary	13.6	11.4	8.8	8.4
some high school	24.7	27.8	18.1	18.0
high school	49.3	38.4	47.5	42.6
some college	5.2	16.0	17.1	19.1
college	1.1	3.2	5.8	7.9
post grad	6.3	3.1	2.6	4.0
Race				
white	69.7	66.8	77.5	77.0
black	26.9	28.4	19.8	20.0
other	3.3	4.8	2.7	3.0
Marital Status				
married	56.0	58.8	60.7	51.5
single	23.2	28.9	13.6	35.7
others	20.8	12.3	25.7	12.9
Sex				
male	42.8	33.2	65.9	54.4
female	57.2	66.8	34.1	45.6
Age				
19	NA	NA	NA	NA
20-24	16.8	17.7	18.7	30.6
25-59	74.4	61.4	76.2	65.4
60+	8.8	20.9	5.2	4.0

****

Source: 1984 and Plant Closing Supplement.

education, sex, and age (see Table 3.10). Other job losers who are discouraged are twice (22.3 percent) as likely to have attended college as displaced discouraged workers (12.6 percent). Displaced discouraged workers are slightly more likely (42.8 percent) to be male than other job losers who are discouraged. Finally, other job losers are much more likely to be 60 years of age or older (20.9 percent) than are the displaced discouraged (8.8 percent).

Officially unemployed workers losing a job for other reasons are dissimilar to discouraged workers on most demographic dimensions, but especially in terms of sex and age. Among displaced workers, the unemployed are much more likely to be males (65.9 percent) than the discouraged (42.8 percent); similarly, among other job losers, males comprise a larger share of the unemployed (54.4 percent) than of the discouraged (33.2 percent). Among displaced workers, the age distributions of the discouraged and the unemployed are nearly identical; among other job losers, younger workers who are unemployed (30.6 percent) outnumber

Table 3.11

Industrial Sectors in which Displaced Discouraged Workers and Discouraged Workers Losing Jobs for Other Reasons Had Last Worked (as percentages)

```
*****************************************************************
```

Sector:	Plant Closing	Other Job Loss
Agriculture	0.4	5.3
Mining	4.0	0.0
Construction	7.2	5.0
Manufacture-Durable	18.4	11.9
Manufacture-Non-durable	29.9	14.6
Transport	1.4	3.3
Communication	2.5	3.3
Utility	0.6	0.0
Wholesale	3.1	3.3
Retail	8.1	23.1
Finance/Insurance/Real Estate	0.0	2.4
Private House Service	0.0	3.9
Business and Repair	0.0	2.8
Personal Service	7.0	1.9
Entertainment & Recreation	0.0	0.7
Hospital	0.5	3.4
Medical/Exc. Hospital	0.0	4.1
Educational	0.0	2.9
Social Service	0.0	2.5
Other Professional	7.6	1.1
Public Administration	9.3	2.9
Armed Forces	0.0	1.5
Totals	100.0	100.0
N	61,000	167,328

```
*****************************************************************
```

Source: 1984 CPS and Plant Closing Supplement.

those who are discouraged (18.7 percent), while older workers who are discouraged (20.9 percent) greatly exceed those who are unemployed (4.0 percent).

Sectoral Employment

Do displaced discouraged workers and other job losers who are discouraged lose jobs from different kinds of industries? Manufacturing, retail, and personal services were the sectors of greatest divergence between the two groups of job losers (see Table 3.11).[14] Displaced discouraged workers were almost twice as likely to have lost a job in manufacturing (48 percent) as those not displaced (27 percent). By contrast, other job losers (23 percent) were nearly three times more likely to be involved in retail-trade job loss than the displaced (8 percent).

These findings make sense on two levels. Manufacturing has declined so precipitously over the last decade that vast numbers of people have been affected. Such structural change helps to explain why displaced discouraged workers are more likley than other discouraged workers to have been employed in manu-facturing. On the other hand, retail trade has been dominated by low-wage, part-time employment—jobs that are also characterized by high voluntary turnover. This would help to account for the association between these occupation groups and job loss for other reasons.

DISCOURAGED WORKERS WHO NEVER WORKED

Ironically, one in seven discouraged workers has never worked. Those who have never worked, desire employment, yet claim that they are not looking for work because they stand little chance of being hired, are considered to be dis-couraged. They are likely to be young people out of high school or college, but some are older people who have few family responsibilities. They may lack marketable skills, have marginal disabilities, or be subject to discrimination for reasons unrelated to their potential worth as employees. Minorities are likely to be overrepresented, at least in the younger age range, because of their higher high school dropout rates. Some may have set unrealistic wage goals or other criteria for employment that the market cannot meet.

Expectations about discouraged workers who never worked were supported by an analysis of their demographics.[15] Six in ten have less than a high school education. Only 40 percent have completed high school. About two-thirds are minorities, mainly blacks (36 percent). Seventy-two percent are not married. Fifty-five percent are males. Some of these characteristics are related to their youth. The "never-worked discouraged" are young: one-half are 24 years of age or younger. None are 60 years of age or older.

The displaced discouraged workers, other job losers who are discouraged, and the discouraged who have never worked have very different demographic profiles (see Table 3.12).[16] The never-worked discouraged are more likely to be poorly educated, to be minorities, especially blacks, to never have been married, to be male, and to be young (20 to 24 years) than either the displaced discouraged or discouraged workers who lost their jobs for other reasons.

These demographic differences imply that the discouraged who lack work experience will have less ability to compete in a highly competitive labor market, even relative to other discouraged workers. As already demonstrated, the dis-couraged with work experience are at a disadvantage relative to the "core" labor force, which is dominated by prime-working-age, educated or skilled, white males. Among discouraged workers only, those who have never worked are likely to be the least competitive subset.

CONCLUSION

This first disaggregated look at the characteristics of discouraged workers suggests that they are a very heterogeneous group. Although a large majority

Table 3.12

Demographic Characteristics of Discouraged Workers Involved in a Plant Closing, Out of Work for Other Reasons, and Never Worked (as percentages)

```
*********************************************************************
Demographic
Category:          Plant Closing   Other Job Loss   Never Worked
---------------------------------------------------------------------

Education
elementary             13.6             11.4            20.1
some high school       24.7             27.8            40.6
high school            49.3             38.4            24.9
some college            5.2             16.0            14.4
college                 1.1              3.2             0.0
post grad               6.3              3.1             0.0

Race
white                  69.7             66.8            34.7
black                  26.9             28.4            50.7
other                   3.3              4.8            14.6

Marital Status
married                56.0             58.8            27.7
single                 23.2             28.9            64.6
other                  20.8             12.3             7.7

Sex
male                   42.8             33.2            54.9
female                 57.2             66.8            45.1

Age
19                      NA               NA              NA
20-24                  16.8             17.7            50.5
25-59                  74.4             61.4            49.5
60+                     8.8             20.9             0.0

N                     61,000          231,043          38,882
*********************************************************************
```

Source: 1984 CPS and Plant Closing Supplement.

have some work experience, relatively few are victims of plant closings or layoffs. Roughly the same proportion are people who have never yet held a job.

The largest group of the discouraged left their last jobs for a wide variety of reasons other than involuntary layoff. Demographically, they resemble the unemployed (those currently looking for work) in some ways, but differ in others, for instance, by including a higher proportion of women. However, demographics alone reveal little about the reasons for their status.

The discouraged claim they want work but believe they will not find the work they want. Just what it would take to get them to work, even to look for work, remains unclear. To answer these questions, it is necessary to look beyond the kinds of information that the Census Bureau surveys provide to information on the discouraged workers' past job experience, their skills and education, desires and motivation, family structure, and current sources of income.

Before examining this new information about discouraged workers, however, it will be useful to review some actual case histories: real people, whose personal histories reveal greater complexity than the standard labor-force categories can capture.

NOTES

1. The absence of extensive analysis should not be blamed on the BLS, which has not been asked to undertake these kinds of analyses by Congress or the executive branch. Its main focus has always been reporting basic data about the labor force.

2. "Displaced workers" are defined, using the CPS 1984 plant-closing supplement, as those who are "no longer working at a job" because: (1) their plant or company closed down or moved; (2) the plant or company was operating but their jobs were lost because of slack work, their position or shift was abolished, or a seasonal job was completed; and (3) their self-operated business failed. Based on answers to the 1984 CPS plant-closing supplement, "other job losers" were defined as those who were not displaced and who answered that they had left their last job for any of the following reasons: (1) personal, family (including pregnancy), or school; (2) health; (3) retirement or old age; (4) seasonal job completed; (5) temporary nonseasonal job completed; (6) unsatisfactory work arrangements (hours, pay, etc.); and (7) other. Other job losers also were not looking for work because of discouragement, measured in the usual way.

Those labeled "never worked" answered that they had never worked to the following question: "When did you last work for pay at a regular job or business, either full- or part-time?"

Details of the survey are provided in: U.S. Bureau of the Census, Data User Services Division, "Technical Documentation: Current Population Survey, January 1984, Displaced Workers" (Washington, D.C.: U.S. Bureau of the Census).

3. Many analyses based on BLS definitions (e.g., Flaim and Seghal 1985) do not classify workers as displaced unless they had held a job for at least three years. Using BLS definitions, only 5 million workers are displaced. In this analysis, no distinctions are made based on job tenure unless stated explicitly.

4. Figures for discouraged workers reported in chapters 1 and 2 are based on annual averages; consequently, monthly data, such as the monthly CPS figures for January 1984, may vary substantially.

The BLS questions on discouragement are always cast in the present tense, that is, "Does [respondent] want a regular job now, either full- or part-time?" followed by "What are the reasons [respondent] is not looking for work?" Discouragement, then, is measured at one point in time. Those questions reveal nothing about changes in discouragement prior to or after questioning. Therefore, BLS data indicate numbers of discouraged workers at any given time, but cannot be used to estimate the total numbers discouraged at one time or another over the course of a year or some other time period. If periods of discouragement are relatively brief, the latter number could be much larger than the former.

5. The demographics of job tenure, however, shed some light on the relationship. If little job experience is defined as having three years or less job tenure, then within this less experienced group, displaced discouraged workers differ from the displaced unemployed and the rehired in terms of age, race, sex, and education. *Age*: One-third of the unemployed (36 percent) and rehired (34 percent) are at least 60 years of age, while nearly two-thirds (62 percent) of the discouraged fall in this age group. *Race*: About two-thirds of the unemployed (67 percent) and rehired (69 percent) are blacks, compared with 82 percent of the discouraged. *Sex*: Although women comprise a high proportion of the unemployed (72 percent) and rehired (69 percent), they are an even higher proportion of the discouraged (87 percent). *Education*: Lower levels of education predominate among the less experienced, especially those with less than a high school diploma. Eighty-six percent of the discouraged, 55 percent of the unemployed, and 50 percent of the rehired had three years or less work experience at a plant that was shut down.

6. Figures are not presented in constant dollars.

7. To examine the relationship of demographic characteristics to earning and employment, workers are divided into those who had earned $200 or less and those who had earned more. *High earnings*: On each demographic dimension, discouraged workers are disadvantaged compared with those who are unemployed or rehired. Discouraged high-wage earners were more likely to be young, minority, female, single, and less educated than are their counterparts in the labor force. *Low earnings*: Those with low earnings differ demographically from those with high earnings. Discouraged workers are more likely to be of prime working age (25 to 59 years), minority, female, widowed or divorced, and less educated.

8. Standard Industrial Classification (SIC) codes were used to classify sectors.

9. This result could be explained by a precipitous decline in nondurable goods production vis-à-vis durable goods production. In Ohio, from 1979 to 1982, for example, nondurable goods production declined 13.5 percent, but durables fell 23.3 percent.

10. Sample sizes were too small to permit valid analysis of respondent demographics.

11. This limitation on the plant-closing experience could bias results for the period from 1977 to 1985, when steelworkers who were laid off from Youngstown Sheet and Tube and did not retire early lost 2.2 jobs on the average over the eight years of the study (Buss and Redburn 1987). Those periodically laid off tended to accept jobs in basic manufacturing that were at risk of being terminated. It may be more important to understand cyclical or sequential patterns of layoffs than to study them at one point in time.

12. See Note 2 for wording of questions and reasons for job loss.

13. Unfortunately, only limited comparisons between the displaced worker

and other job losers are possible. Although considerable information on displaced workers was gathered by the 1974 plant-closing supplement, comparable information on other job losers is gathered only for the monthly CPS and, therefore, is not available for comparison.

14. Occupational differences did not stand out between the two discouraged worker groups having work experience, with the possible exception of machine operators. Displaced discouraged workers (22 percent) are nearly twice as likely as others (12 percent) to lose machine operator jobs.

15. There were 71,239 discouraged workers who had never worked in the unweighted monthly CPS sample.

16. The monthly CPS includes information on respondents aged 16 years and older. The 1984 plant-closing supplement, however, "screened out" all those respondents aged 19 years or younger, so that no information on plant-closing experiences of younger people was gathered. To ensure comparability across ages for the displaced, other job losers, and those who have never worked, 20 years of age was chosen as a cutoff. Fixing the cutoff age at 20 years or older reduces the number of "never-worked discouraged" individuals available for analysis from 71,239 to 38,882.

4 *PROFILES IN DISCOURAGEMENT*

Behind the statistics are real people. Categorized as discouraged workers by their responses to a few questions and further categorized by our analysis in terms of their work experience and reasons for leaving their last jobs, the people thus labeled arrive at a common status by varied routes. Moreover, as they are questioned further about their personal histories, reasons for joblessness, and ambitions, the neatness of the categories is exposed as being oversimplified.[1]

The cases[2] presented in this chapter take us beyond the caricatures that survey analysis necessarily fosters, and they represent a first step in reconstructing and enriching our understanding of this group of potential workers.

DISPLACED DISCOURAGED WORKERS

We have observed that only a small minority of the discouraged—even in a community that has recently experienced massive job losses due to the closing of large manufacturing facilities—fit the classic image of the discouraged worker as someone who lost a job involuntarily, who subsequently searched for work as one of the "unemployed" and who, finding nothing, eventually gave up the search.

The first set of cases presented here are people who fit this image in the essentials; yet their work histories, experiences since they were laid off, and especially their views on what it will take for them to work again raise questions about the meaning or usefulness of this category. John, Ray, and Henry are all experienced skilled workers whose jobs ended—three, five, and six years ago, respectively—in a plant closing or work-force cutback. They are thus "displaced'' as well as ''discouraged,'' by the standard classification criteria. The subsequent responses of each differ, however; although each intends or intended to return to work when first interviewed and classified, factors not recognized in the standard classification have complicated their return to the labor force. John's abandonment of the search for a new job is apparently part of a deep-seated psychological pattern that predates his layoff. Likewise, Ray's temporary withdrawal from active job search was more than a reaction to the difficulty of finding new work; it was also part of a profound and painful adjustment to the loss of a proud status and identity as a craftsman. Henry's ''discouragement'' is complicated not only by deep cynicism and pessimism but also by his ''unofficial'' employment in criminal activity subsequent to his layoff. Applied to each of these cases, it seems the categories of discouragement and displacement are only superficially appropriate and not very useful in helping us to understand what they want from a job or, from a public policy perspective, what they need.

Jack

Jack, 50 years old, is married to a school teacher and has two children, ages 8 and 13. Three years ago, Jack lost his job of 20 years when the metal-fabricating plant where he was a forklift operator closed after a labor dispute.

Jack blames the plant closing on younger workers without a stake in the company who made unreasonable demands, eventually forcing the owner to sell out. When a new owner reopened the facility, Jack expected to be called back to work because of his seniority and supportive attitude toward the company. However, he was not called back. In fact, few former employees were. Jack believes his age was the deciding factor.

At first, Jack applied for only a few jobs. He kept harboring the feeling that he would be called back. After some months, he developed severe chest pains and was rushed to the hospital several times. Periodic visits to specialists found nothing wrong.

Jack was regarded by neighbors as a hypochondriac long before his layoff. He frequently missed work for one kind of illness or another. He also missed work around the home. For years, Jack complained of fatigue, allergies, chest pains, insomnia, and other diseases. Frequent visits to specialized clinics always left him with a clean bill of health.

Jack, through most of his life, was obsessive even about the most minor things. His lawn had to be cut frequently in just a certain way. Garbage had to be neatly packaged and taped. Living quarters were sparkling clean, with each thing in its place.

Although Jack insisted on neatness, he frequently found ways to avoid doing the work himself, preferring to pass the responsibility on to others, whom he would carefully and annoyingly instruct so that his expectations could be achieved.

Jack has now sunk into a deep depression. He rarely leaves the house, doesn't even watch television, and always appears to have a three-day growth of beard. He has given up visiting friends and neighbors. He does little housework because of his chest pains.

Gradually, in the past year, Jack has become alienated from his wife and children. He is quiet most of the time, with an occasional angry outburst. His children show no outward signs of distress, but his wife frequently runs to close friends in tears.

Fortunately for Jack's family, his wife earns enough as a school teacher to maintain their desired quality of life. Rather than helping psychologically, however, this adds fuel to the fire: Jack probably feels emasculated by his wife's relatively successful career.

The prospects for Jack do not seem good. Because he sees his illnesses as physical, he will not consider seeking psychiatric help. Nor will he see the family priest.

Ray

Ray, who is 60 years old, gave up a good job five years ago rather than leave his hometown. Ray's wife works for the local government. His two grown children have left but remain close by in the area.

Ray spent his 20s and 30s working on farms, in lumberyards, and on construction crews. Although never a union member, he was proficient at carpentry, electrical wiring, plastering, and several other trades. He built the house in which he lived until quite recently.

After moving from job to job, Ray settled into a highly skilled craftsman position where he could use all of his trades and be his own boss, even though working for a large corporation. In this job, which he held for 15 years, Ray achieved status as an artisan. His work became well-known as one of the best at his craft.

When Ray, at 55, was at the peak of his career, his company was acquired by another. He was told that to keep his job he would have to move. Although Ray had traveled widely in his life, he had never moved more than 500 yards from where he was born. His land, relatives, friends, and entire life were tied to this small corner of the world.

Ray weighed his options. He concluded that leaving town, which would force his wife to give up her job, was not a fair trade for keeping his. Ray's employment was terminated.

In a few days, Ray went into a deep depression. He became quiet and withdrawn. He stayed home most of the time, except for an occasional visit to his old job site.

People familiar with Ray's skills encouraged him to set up his own business, but he could not see himself as the manager of his own firm; nor did he know anyone with whom a business partnership sounded like a good idea.

Eventually, Ray found a job that seemed comparable to the one he lost.

However, the job was a "rip-off." It paid on a project-by-project basis. It had no benefits. It demanded long hours. Workers supplied their own tools. Ray figured he was earning about the minimum wage. Sometimes he even came out behind: he would pay for materials out of his own pocket so as not to disappoint customers. Ray worked at this job for nearly two years and would have stayed longer, but the business folded.

Ray took on small handyman projects for the next two years. One day, an acquaintance from his old job offered him a caretaker position. Although not related in any way to his skills, he took to the job, in his words, "like a duck to water."

Now he is working and lives his old life. The only exception: he has moved five miles down the road.

Henry

Henry is 58 years old. He is divorced and has five grown children. He once worked in a manufacturing plant as a machinist; he was the first and only black man, he says, to work there as a machinist. He has not worked officially since being laid off in a 1981 work-force reduction.

Henry now gets his money from occasional odd jobs. He has also "run numbers," until caught by the FBI, who confiscated one of his three cars. He asks why the state can run the lottery, but he cannot run numbers.

There are two counts against his getting a job now, Henry says. He is old and he is black. So, he does not bother to apply for jobs. He says that even if he did try to get a machinist's job, he would need to take a refresher course.

Henry's first job was in the military service from 1947 to 1954. He was not honorably discharged, "because he was black." He did no work officially again until 1973. In 1972, he enrolled in a publicly funded training course that allowed him to get a job a year later at a metal-forming mill. In 1976, he lost his job for reasons that are unclear. He says it was because he is black. In 1978, Henry got the job from which he was laid off in 1981.

Henry liked his work at the forming mill, especially the varied tasks and the emphasis on skill. "Quantity" was not as imporatnt as "quality." But he says he had a mental block about that work because of all the prejudice to which he felt exposed.

Henry believes that most people do not give him a chance to show his abilities. As he sees things, blacks get degrading jobs. Most are forced into welfare because that is better than low-paying work. After a couple of generations, blacks "don't know how to work anymore. All they know is welfare."

Henry says there is no need to work if you are going to be tired and hungry because the pay is so low. You may as well just be hungry. Henry wants to make a fair living, but believes he won't get the chance.

LEFT WORK FOR OTHER REASONS

The group comprising the majority of discouraged workers, those who were not victims of a plant closing or layoff but have worked before, is likely to be even more diverse than the displaced group. Two out of three are women. Wilma, Sandy, and Cheryl are experienced workers who were not displaced, but reported that they were discouraged from looking for work when first interviewed. Wilma worked steadily for 15 years, quit work to have children, and has not worked since, although her children are now well into their twenties. There seems to be a large gap between the kind of job that she would accept and the kind of work she is likely to find. Sandy has experience as a cook, but lost her last steady job four years ago when she developed serious health problems. Her prospects are limited not only by continued poor health and a narrow range of job skills, but also because she has limited her search to the kind of work she has done before. Cheryl, the youngest of the three, has worked only part-time and briefly since finishing high school. She seems to have abandoned her search for new work in part because she prefers to be at home with her two young children; yet she clearly enjoys work and has some skills that employers would value. In all three cases, the women are living with someone who provides the household with income. None of the three displays great urgency about finding a job, despite their obvious desire to work again under what they regard as ideal or attractive conditions.

Wilma

Wilma worries about being dependent on her husband's income. It seems that she is preparing herself for the possibility of losing him and having to support herself. She talks often of how her life would be different if she were a widow.

When she married, Wilma had worked for 12 years as a telephone operator. After working three more years, she quit to have children. Although her children are now grown, she has not worked since.

Working was a positive experience for Wilma. She liked the people she worked with, and she liked helping the public. Different shifts allowed her some flexibility. She enjoyed the job.

Being a homemaker while Wilma's two daughters were young was rewarding, but now that they are grown she feels that housekeeping is useless. She says she would like to work, but that her age, lack of experience, and the time she has been out of the labor force prevent her from getting a job, especially in the line of work that interests her: retail sales.

When she goes to the mall, Wilma looks in store windows for help-wanted signs. She does not want to work just anywhere, so only looks at certain stores. Even when she sees signs, she does not always apply. Wilma has the impression that stores put out signs but do not really hire anyone. She always sees the same sales people in the stores. When she does apply, no one ever calls her back.

Sometimes the applications have questions listed that, she says, should not be there, such as: "How will this income be used?" She takes this to mean, "If this income will not be the sole support of the family, you don't need the job."

Wilma gets discouraged sometimes; she feels like she is "in Russia." Employers think that she does not need a job because her husband works, so they won't hire her.

Wilma's daughters (ages 24 and 26) both live at home. Both are unemployed. Sometimes she wonders why she sent them to school. It seems like all employers want experienced rather than formally educated workers. Her daughters are continually told: "If you only had experience, I'd hire you right away."

Wilma likes to have a routine, so her days are pretty much the same. She gets up early and fills her days with cleaning, laundry, shopping, cooking, and watching television or reading. Occasionally, she needlepoints or arranges flowers.

When asked what her dream job would consist of, Wilma says she would like to be the co-owner of a business, such as a woman's clothing store or a gift shop. She realizes that she does not have the knowledge or experience to be the sole owner, and she does not have the capital. If she had a partner, Wilma would not have to be there all the time and would be able to get away from the business if she wanted to. She would like to earn about $35,000, plus bonuses. She would like vacation and hospitalization benefits, too.

At the same time, Wilma thinks that she will have a difficult time, at best, even finding a part-time job with no benefits, paying the minimum wage.

Sandy

Although she has not worked in over four years, Sandy would like a job. Sandy lives with her son in a commercial area. Their house's exterior needs some repair, and broken furniture litters the porch. Inside, broken television sets and stuffed animals abound.

Sandy is angry. She makes it clear that in her view our society has discriminated against her. The employment system does not work for minorities, she says. Although she wants to work, no one is interested in hiring a 41-year-old black woman with a medical problem.

Sandy was trained to be a cook, like her father and uncle. She worked at other jobs before she found this kind of work, first as a barmaid in a bowling alley when she was 19 for four years and then at a bar for a year.

After that, she found employment as a salad girl at a restaurant. Sandy liked working there and was promoted to head cook after a short time. She worked at the restaurant for four years, but then it was sold and the new owner replaced most of the employees.

She was unemployed for two years, then found a job as a cook at a community center. Sandy worked there for four years, but had to leave because of poor health. It was painful for her to stand for long periods of time at work. She took medicine to help relieve the pain, but it also made her too sleepy to work. Sandy left the job in 1980 because of her illness and has had only a few part-time jobs since then. In 1983, she was diagnosed as having arthritis in her knees, legs, ankles, and feet.

Cooking is the only thing Sandy wants to do. She does not want to be a secretary sitting behind a desk with someone telling her what to do all the time. She likes the freedom of cooking. It is more like a hobby than a job, she says. People talk to her about retraining, but Sandy just wants to cook.

If Sandy could get a job, she says she would not take the medicine that makes her sleepy. A job would be worth the extra pain. Each week she goes to the state employment service office and puts her name in for jobs that interest her. Each time, she is told that she will be called, but calls never come. She finds this degrading. She would have employers interview on the spot. "That way at least you'd get an interview; you wouldn't get eliminated because of your race." Also, she believes that "if someone says you'll get a call, you should get one, even if you don't get the job."

Sandy wants to know why it is so hard for someone like her, who wants to work, to get a job and earn a living. "The government just hands out money to some people." Sandy has a brother who committed a crime and was placed in an asylum for a short time. Because he was classified as mentally disturbed, the government will give him a monthly Supplemental Security Income (SSI) payment for the rest of his life. She notes that his payment "for committing a crime" is more than she can get on general relief. Sandy wrote a letter to the president about this, and the reply indicated that she should apply for disability because of her medical condition. She did so but was found not eligible. As her condition worsened, she applied three more times but was denied each time.

Her life is a quiet one. Each day she gets up at 6:00 A.M., does exercises, watches the news, washes up, then eats breakfast. Because her medicine makes her sleepy, she only takes it every other day. If her doctor knew that, he would be upset. So, some days she cleans and watches television; other days she takes her medicine then sleeps most of the day. She likes to work crossword puzzles and collects stuffed turtles, which fill her living room.

When Sandy's friends go out to lunch to celebrate a birthday, they always invite her, but she can never go because there is not enough money. This is when she feels most discouraged.

Sandy dreams of owning a restaurant. She says if she "hits the lotto," she'll buy an empty restaurant near her home and turn it into a soul food kitchen. It would take some time to turn a profit, but Sandy would be in charge: she would have her own menu, her own specials, and no one would be telling her what to do. She realizes her chances are slim and that she probably will never work as a cook again.

Cheryl

Cheryl just finished her first job since high school. From January to July 1987, she took care of a woman with multiple sclerosis who lived across the street from her. Cheryl was paid $20 a day for working four hours. She fed and gave medicine to the woman, kept the house clean, did laundry, and also took care of the woman's retarded son when he was home. The neighbors wanted Cheryl to work for them full-time, but she has three school-age children (two sons and a daughter) who need her attention too. The neighbors found a full-time helper, so Cheryl is not working now.

Taking care of her neighbor was more than just a job for Cheryl. Tears came to her eyes as Cheryl described her neighbor's condition and difficulty in living. Cheryl talked about her constant efforts at reinforcing her neighbor's dignity: it is hard for a woman who can't do anything for herself to feel that she has control over her life and home. Cheryl left all decisions to her neighbor and acted as her neighbor's legs and arms.

Cheryl is constantly busy. During the school year, she volunteers at the school and works with students learning how to use microcomputers. She and her husband are also involved in the soccer league in her area. Cheryl's kitchen was filled with new soccer equipment. The league has computerized some of its functions, and Cheryl is interested in getting more involved in this phase of the league's operations.

When she isn't busy with school or soccer, Cheryl drives her mother on errands, works in her vegetable garden, or works in the yard. Her latest efforts involve ripping out an old hedge and planting a flower garden with the help of her son.

Cheryl talked about her very first job, as a stock person in the men's clothing section of a discount department store. She was in high school at the time, but the department manager gave her a lot of responsibility. The pay was very low. Cheryl said she was the only one at the store who really wanted to work. Other employees were always going ''on break'' and leaving her to watch three, four, or even five departments at a time.

After high school, Cheryl got married and quit her job. She and her husband began a family right away. Her husband had a good job, so with young children to care for, Cheryl did not look for work outside the home.

At the time of her first interview, Cheryl's husband was temporarily laid off. She was especially discouraged then about not being able to get a job, because her family really needed the income. She really wanted to get a job to help out, but found that her lack of experience kept her from getting any job.

Now, Cheryl looks at the jobs listed in the paper every Sunday. Sometimes she even calls to find out more about a job. She is especially interested in working as a baker. However, it seems to her that every employer wants experienced workers, although Cheryl likes to bake and decorate her own cakes, she has no formal experience as a baker. She knows that, if she could get a job, she could do whatever they want her to do. Right now, with her husband back on the job, Cheryl is not seriously looking—just ''watching out.'' Her youngest boy gets out of school earlier than his brother or sister and cannot stay at home alone, so Cheryl feels she can't get a job until he is a little older, maybe in two or three years.

Cheryl says she will seriously look for work then. She would like to learn more about computers so that she can use them in whatever job she gets. She and her husband will be buying a personal computer soon, so she will get some practice. Cheryl says machines will be the laborers of the future, so she has to stay away from "labor" jobs.

In a dream that she has had several times, Cheryl sees herself working at a drafting firm doing technical drawings. She is paid very well and only has to work part of the year. Cheryl doesn't think this exact dream will come true, but she does believe she will be working some day in a technical job that will pay well and still allow time for her family.

HAVE NEVER WORKED

Among those labeled as discouraged workers are people who have never worked. Some, it is safe to say, have never looked for work, although their answers to the standard survey questions suggest that they would like a job. Most in this group are quite young; among these are people who plan to return to school before entering the labor force. Ron and Fred, both classified as discouraged, are black teenagers who are one year from high school graduation. Elyse, on the other hand, has left school but had no success in finding a job. By her own testimony, she may be unable to accept the discipline and responsibility that employment would require.

Ron

Next year Ron will be a senior in high school. He lives at home with his parents and a brother and sister. Both of his parents work. His dad manages a bar, and his mother works for a utility company. Ron's older brother recently got a job with a car dealer.

Ron has never worked but says he would like to. He could use the money. A while back, Ron picked up an application at Burger King, but he has not taken it in yet because he must first apply for his Social Security number. All he wants is a part-time job that pays minimum wage—no benefits, nothing like that, probably just a clean-up job. But it is "hard to get a job around here." He has no car with which to get to work.

Ron likes school, being with his friends, and taking classes. After he graduates, Ron will try to find a job, but he says he will have to leave the area to find one. He is thinking about going to Nevada; he wants to see what it's like out there.

Basketball is Ron's favorite sport. He likes to play it and watch it on television. Next year he will go out for the school team. He has no other hobbies.

Ron says he is not discouraged by not finding or having a job this summer.

He will spend his summer days sleeping in, sitting around listening to music, and doing things with his friends.

Fred

Fred is 17 years old. He got his first job when he was ten and has had two jobs since then. His first work was cleaning up a local automotive store, but after three years, the company moved to the south side of town and Fred had no way to get there. Later the same year, Fred got a temporary summer job as stock boy in a local wine shop. The following summer, he found a job at a local restaurant, but the restaurant closed. Fred has not worked since then, but he has applied for jobs at several food stores and hamburger places.

Working can be fun, Fred says. He does not like to be "lazy." Fred liked working at the automotive store because he was around a lot of men, and they were always talking about cars. He did not make much, just the minimum wage, but he liked it. Being a stock boy at the wine shop was fun too, because his friends could come in and talk while he worked. Working at a restaurant was different; he was not supposed to talk to anyone, just go around and clean things up.

Fred says he wants a job now and would take less than the minimum wage. All he wants to earn is about $50 a week. Benefits are not important, but he would like to know that the job won't get "cut off," like it has before. Although he wants a job, he does not think of himself as discouraged. It does not bother him not to have a job, but if he had one he would buy clothes and a car.

Next year Fred will be a senior in high school. He likes school. History is his favorite subject.

Fred wants to join the military service when he is out of school. He wants to be a Green Beret, then a recruiter. Fred wants a challenge. He has seen movies of Green Berets, and he likes what they do.

Eventually Fred would like to marry and have a family. It would be nice to have someone to go home to and to have kids to play with.

Fred doesn't like Youngstown. It's too small. He has visited in the Carolinas—Charlotte and Greenville—and liked it there. He has a lot of family there. There are more jobs; more women, too.

Yet the perfect place to live would be in Beverly Hills. Fred would like to own a store there, selling jewelry or clothes. He could "come out on top" and be rich. If he got really rich, he would not have to work.

If Fred doesn't get a job this summer, he will help his parents out at home and play basketball with his friends.

Elyse

A woman in her 20s, Elyse has never held a full-time job.

Elyse's father left home when she was very young. Her mother raised her alone, supported by public assistance. Elyse's mother subjected her to continual criticism.

About the time that Elyse turned 20 years old, her mother, without explanation, moved Elyse's few belongings out on the front lawn of their home and told her to get out.

Elyse stayed with different friends until either she or her friends had had enough of one another. Eventually, she met a man who was kind to her and moved in with him. The man and Elyse lived in a basement apartment in his parents' home.

While in this relationship, Elyse tried to find work but was largely unsuccessful. She has held only part-time babysitting jobs. Elyse says that having no work may be her fault. She will not work regular hours, prefers to come and go as she pleases, and cannot tolerate not having at least one weekday and the weekend off. Elyse also believes that she is just a "little slow" and cannot hold a responsible job.

CONCLUSION

What does this small group of individual profiles reveal or suggest about the nature of discouragement? Certainly, it demonstrates that the label discouraged worker covers such a broad range of possibilities that it is of limited value as a guide to policymaking. Nor does the three-fold division of the discouraged into displaced workers, others with job experience, and those with no experience provide much information about why these groups are not only unemployed, but also not actively searching for work. Finally, it is worth noting that for several of those interviewed, discouragement is just a way station, as they move back and forth between employment, unemployment, school, or child-care responsibilities. Yet, while their official job statuses may vary from day to day, the factors that limit their prospects of finding and holding good jobs do not change. This is a point to which we will return in later chapters, when discussing public policies that could benefit this group.

More information is needed about the motives and attitudes, economic circumstances, physical and emotional health, skills, education, and goals of an individual before deciding what it would take to get that person into a job. Only when we have developed that depth of information about discouraged workers as a whole group, or about parts of the group, will we have an adequate information base for answering the most basic public policy question: Can we develop cost-effective programs to help some or all discouraged workers prepare for and find employment? The following chapters present some of the information needed to answer this question—information that until now has been unavailable.

NOTES

1. Some respondents interviewed in greater depth for the case studies reported having looked for work fairly recently. Discouraged workers are defined as those not actively searching for a job within the last four weeks.

2. Case-study respondents were selected from those who had completed the structured survey questionnaires in the Youngstown studies. No systematic procedures were followed in making case-study selections other than to seek individuals who appeared to represent varied paths to discouragement. Interviewers used a less structured interview format, covering topics ranging from work experience to expectations and motivation, but allowing respondents maximum freedom to respond. Interviews averaged one hour to complete. In a few instances, others acquainted with the individual were also interviewed.

5   *COPING WITHOUT WORK*

Even if they are not officially "unemployed," discouraged workers are jobless, and thus have no earned income—at least none that they will acknowledge. They must obtain their income, if any, from other sources. Oddly, though, to our knowledge no research as been conducted on how they subsist. Are discouraged workers primarily dependent on government transfer payments to survive? Or, do most have some other source of income, say, from other family members?

Published research, based on Bureau of Labor Statistics (BLS) special topic and standard monthly Current Population Survey (CPS) interviews, has focused almost entirely on barriers to worker participation in the labor force. The monthly CPS, for example, asks respondents only why they are not looking for work.[1]

By examining how discouraged workers cope without jobs, we can add to the insights on barriers to their work participation provided by the standard surveys. Some would argue that, if people in households receiving government transfer payments, such as Aid to Families with Dependent Children (AFDC), Supplemental Security Income (SSI), and Social Security, want jobs, are able to work, but are not looking for work, and in many cases, do not intend to look, then perhaps social policy is promoting dependency. Others would argue that such payments, combined with any other sources of household income, are usually inadequate to provide a decent living standard and therefore do not reward dependency. They would stress barriers to participation that could be remedied by job preparation and placement, perhaps supplemented by subsidized job creation.

If people out of work are members of families that allow them to live fairly comfortably without working, then they may be fairly selective in accepting jobs, not only with regard to wage or salary, but also hours, benefits, and job satisfaction. In whatever way they are classified by the standard surveys, if people do not want to take jobs that provide reasonable rewards, then it is unreasonable to regard their lack of employment as a failure of social policy; nor is it clear that any public policy should be developed to meet their limited desire or need for work.

Data from the 1984 Survey of Income and Program Participation (SIPP) are now available to answer questions about discouraged worker sources and levels of income. In 1984 SIPP was the first in a continuing series of national surveys conducted by the Census Bureau to measure income sources and the use of government programs. The survey's longitudinal design will eventually allow researchers to track individual and family income and income sources over periods up to two and one-half years. This chapter reports the results of our analysis of the SIPP data, along with similar information from the Youngstown area survey.

This chapter is organized around answers to the following questions:

1. How many discouraged workers receive income even though they are jobless? If so, how much do they receive and where does it come from?

2. What is the role of other family or household income in providing support for discouraged workers? How many family members provide support? How much support is available? Where do families obtain their income? Typically, how important is the discouraged worker's income or lack of income to the family?

3. How important are government cash and noncash benefits to discouraged workers and their families?

4. How do discouraged workers perceive their own financial situation? How do their families manage their finances?

POSSIBLE ANSWERS

Most Americans can scarcely imagine survival without wage or salary income. About 7 percent of adult heads of household nationally work for wages just to survive at or below federal poverty levels (Danziger and Gottschalk 1986). Yet, more than 1 million discouraged workers, in any given year, have dropped out of the competition to find jobs and live without earned income. How do they survive?

At any given point in time, a discouraged worker may be supported by one or more sources of unearned income. First, those recently laid off from jobs may qualify for and receive unemployment benefits, including unemployment insurance, union supplemental unemployment benefits (SUB pay), and federal Trade Adjustment Assistance (TAA). These benefits may provide a discouraged worker with steady income for between six and 12 months after a job is terminated.

Second, those whose families are destitute may receive welfare benefits, such as AFDC, state general relief (GR), or SSI. In addition to transfer payments, discouraged workers may be eligible for federal noncash benefit programs, such as Medicaid, food stamps, subsidized school lunches (for their children), and subsidized housing.

Third, discouraged workers who are not receiving public subsidies may be members of families in which other members provide support from their income.

Fourth, a discouraged worker may have income from a variety of other non-wage sources. Possibilities include rent, a pension from a forced early retirement or from Social Security, or a partial disability pension.

A final possibility is income from work in the hidden or underground economy. Some discouraged workers or members of their households may be employed "off the books." Other "work" involves criminal activities and thus goes unreported.

Merely classifying discouraged workers by sources of financial support provides only a static view of their financial situation. If discouraged workers, like the welfare and working-poor populations, move periodically into and out of the work force, then we need also to take a more dynamic view of their incomes and work status.

The Panel Survey of Income Dynamics, a national study of income dynamics for heads of households from 1968 to 1979, conducted by the University of Michigan (Duncan et al. 1984), found that over the decade, one-fourth of household heads were living in poverty or were on welfare. However, less than 2 percent spent the entire decade in poverty or on welfare. Only 5 percent spent eight of ten years in poverty or on welfare. No comparable long-term longitudinal studies of discouraged workers exist, but it is reasonable to expect that most of them, too, will alternate between periods of earned income and spells of discouragement.

INCOME

The following analysis looks first at the discouraged worker's personal income and sources of income, and second at the income and income sources of the entire household. Methodological issues related to income are discussed in the Appendix.

Personal Income

Being out of work in America seldom means receiving no income. In 1984, nearly three-fifths of discouraged workers had at least some personal income on which to live during the month when they were interviewed (see Table 5.1).[2]

Table 5.1
Individual Income for Discouraged and Unemployed Workers (as percentages)

****

Monthly Income ($):	Discouraged	Unemployed
0	39.9	44.9
1-100	25.6	19.3
101-200	7.0	5.5
201-300	5.6	6.4
301-400	5.5	5.6
401-500	3.9	4.4
501-600	3.5	3.9
601+	9.0	10.0
Totals	100.0	100.0

****

Source: 1984 SIPP.

About the same proportion of the officially unemployed also had some personal income during the month.

In most cases, however, the personal incomes of discouraged and unemployed workers were insufficient to meet basic needs. Nearly three-fourths of both the discouraged (73 percent) and unemployed (70 percent) received $200 or less during the month. The discouraged and the unemployed were in equally poor straits, then, even though the groups differ a great deal demographically (see chapters 2 and 3.)

The sources from which discouraged workers derive their income explain why it cannot provide for even basic needs (see Table 5.2). The largest group receives pension income either from Social Security, private companies or plans, and government agencies. The next largest group are those on welfare, which can, in turn, be placed in three subgroups: (1) those receiving AFDC, the welfare program primarily for women under 40 and supporting a family; (2) those on general relief, who are mainly young males, and largely minority; and (3) those receiving SSI, that is, the disabled. A much smaller group rely on unemployment insurance benefits. Sources of income for the remaining groups are fragmented: child support and alimony, life insurance, casual earnings too small to report, private charity, friends, or workers' compensation. Many use federal food stamps to supplement other, very meager sources of income.

Table 5.2

Numbers of Discouraged Workers with Each Income Source

****

| Source: | Sources Named: | | | |
	First	Second	Third	Total
Social Security	341,030	3,891	0	344,921
Supplemental Security Income (SSI)	25,174	34,023	0	59,197
Unemployment Compensation	76,374	12,037	0	88,411
Veterans Compensation	30,908	17,905	4,333	53,146
Workers Compensation	6,254	0	0	6,254
Aid Dependent Children (AFDC)	280,508	7,281	0	287,789
General Assistance	41,842	63,371	0	105,213
Women Infants Children (WIC)	13,994	12,415	27,920	54,329
Food Stamps	121,109	268,980	26,559	416,648
Child Support Payments	7,904	8,819	8,020	24,743
Alimony	4,332	4,099	4,210	12,641
Private Pension	24,199	74,446	7,890	106,535
Government Pension	6,698	17,158	16,446	40,302
Estate, Trusts	8,175	4,889	0	13,064
Other Retirement	4,306	0	0	4,306
Relatives, Friends	44,017	3,024	0	47,043
National Guard, Reserve	5,717	0	0	5,717
Casual Earnings	15,999	0	0	15,999
Other Cash	20,508	0	0	20,508
Life Insurance	8,119	3,896	0	12,015
Supplemental Unemployment Benefits	4,333	0	0	4,333

****

Source: 1984 SIPP.

Note: Percentages were not calculated because categories of income were not mutually exclusive--respondents were permitted to report up to ten income sources. Also, because income sources were limited, not all income may have been reported.

Importance of Family

Discouraged workers, if forced to rely on their individual incomes, would be among the poorest of the poor, but many receive support from others in their family.[3] To sort out how discouraged workers make ends meet, it is first necessary to determine whether they are single or members of families.[4] The single person must "go it alone." As a member of a family, a discouraged worker may have support from others, but it is also possible that other family members require rather than provide support.

Discouraged workers are primarily members of families (see Table 5.3): only two percent are individuals not living with relatives.[5] It is probably significant that unemployed people are six times more likely than discouraged workers to be living apart from relatives. Those who cannot turn to other family members for support have little choice but to continue searching for a job; therefore, they continue to be classified as unemployed.

Of both discouraged and unemployed workers who are members of a family, two-thirds belong to families with at least three members, as is the case with

Table 5.3
Family Size, Income, and Income Source of Discouraged and Unemployed Workers (as percentages)

Item:	National	
	Discouraged	Unemployed
Family Size(a)		
Not in a family	2.1	11.8
2	21.3	17.4
3-4	37.3	42.5
5+	29.3	28.3
Monthly Family Income(b)		
$ 0- 100	7.4	9.9
$ 100- 300	7.2	9.4
$ 300- 500	8.4	10.6
$ 501- 700	8.3	9.6
$ 701- 900	7.6	8.0
$ 901-1,500	18.7	17.2
$1,501-3,000	28.3	24.1
$3,001+	14.0	11.4
Family Income Source(c)		
SS, AFDC, Earnings	0.6	0.7
SS, AFDC	1.3	1.2
SS, Earnings	8.1	7.1
AFDC, Earnings	3.9	3.0
SS only	12.5	7.6
AFDC only	9.3	8.6
Earnings	53.8	51.9
Other income(d)	10.6	20.0

Source: 1984 SIPP.

a Number of persons in family unit.

b Annual income computed on monthly reported income.

c Major income sources and selected combinations. Categories are mutually exclusive.

d Includes unemployment compensation, pensions, rent, investments.

most American families. A majority, then, has someone to rely on, or alternatively, someone to support.

Forty-two percent of the discouraged workers are members of families with incomes of at least $1,500 a month or $18,000 a year. Others receive substantially less: about one-fourth report income of $500 or below. The incomes of unemployed worker families are distributed in roughly the same pattern.

Most families of discouraged workers have some earned income. Fifty-four percent depend entirely on wages or salaries for their support. Another 12 percent have at least one wage earner in the family but also have another source of income.

Table 5.4

**Demographic Characteristics of Discouraged and Unemployed Workers by
Income Source (as percentages)**

****

Demographic:	Wage		Social Security		AFDC		Total	
	Disc	Unem	Disc	Unem	Disc	Unem	Disc	Unem
Education								
elementary	5.3	7.0	18.9	16.4	12.1	14.1	9.1	8.1
some high school	43.9	25.4	22.6	25.9	40.2	38.5	39.2	27.5
high school	30.8	42.3	39.8	33.5	41.3	34.0	34.4	40.1
some college	13.6	17.2	12.5	17.3	4.9	12.0	11.8	16.7
college	4.5	4.7	5.2	5.2	0.0	1.4	3.9	4.8
post grad	2.0	3.4	0.8	1.7	1.5	0.0	1.6	2.8
Race								
white	77.3	77.3	76.2	64.8	46.9	55.2	70.6	71.4
black	18.2	18.6	23.8	31.7	34.0	40.0	25.2	24.9
Sex								
male	40.7	49.9	50.8	65.2	33.3	35.0	42.7	52.0
female	59.3	50.1	49.2	34.8	66.7	65.0	57.3	48.0
Age								
19	46.2	20.8	9.8	8.6	16.4	6.2	15.0	15.6
20-24	15.5	22.4	8.5	15.8	22.9	24.6	16.4	21.2
25-59	35.6	54.2	23.6	49.7	59.3	68.5	59.7	57.9
60+	2.6	2.7	58.1	25.9	1.4	0.7	8.8	5.3
Marital Status								
married	34.0	48.9	29.8	23.6	28.4	27.0	31.6	38.9
single	61.8	45.3	31.7	46.0	49.9	42.4	54.6	45.0
other	4.2	5.8	38.5	30.4	21.7	30.6	13.8	16.1

****

Source: 1984 SIPP.

Note: Three major income categories were selected for presentation.
       They account for 75 percent of income sources. Income categories
       are mutually exclusive.

Aside from wages, Social Security and AFDC payments account for most
discouraged worker family incomes. Thirteen percent rely exclusively on Social
Security and 9 percent rely exclusively on AFDC. Nearly one-fourth (23 percent)
of the families have at least one Social Security recipient as a member, while
15 percent have a member receiving AFDC. Only 2 percent of the discouraged
worker families report receiving any unemployment insurance benefits, implying
that most household members who do not work have been out of work for some
time, did not work long enough to qualify for benefits, or have never worked.

The families of unemployed workers (see Table 5.4) generally receive income
from the same sources as those of discouraged workers. Earnings from wages
predominate, but some families rely on Social Security or AFDC. Unemployed
worker families are seven times more likely than those of the discouraged,
however, to be receiving unemployment insurance. This is unsurprising, given
that discouraged workers are both less likely to have had long job tenure and

more likely to have been out of work long enough to have exhausted any un-employment benefits for which they were eligible.

Sources of family income vary with the demographic characteristics of discouraged workers, as follows:

- Race: Black households including a discouraged worker are more likely to receive income from AFDC (34 percent) than are those of all discouraged workers (25 percent)

- Sex: Two-thirds of families including a female discouraged worker receive AFDC income, compared with 57 percent having a male discouraged worker.

- Age: Discouraged workers who are under 20 years old account for nearly one-half (46 percent) of those in wage-earning families, although this group constitutes just 15 percent of the discouraged worker population. By contrast, prime-working-age people (25 to 59 years old), who account for 60 percent of all discouraged workers, account for just 36 percent of those in wage-earning families. Those 60 years of age or older account for most (58 percent) of the families receiving Social Security income, although they constitute only 9 percent of all discouraged workers.

- Marital status: Widowed, divorced, or separated discouraged workers are disproportionately likely to be in households receiving Social Security: 39 percent versus 14 percent of all discouraged worker families.

Family versus Individual Income

To understand the importance of family income in supporting discouraged workers, it is necessary to compare the proportion contributed by the discouraged worker (whether earned or not) with that contributed by other family members. If the discouraged worker could substantially contribute to family income by working, then that person's absence from the labor force constitutes a substantial economic loss for the family. In these cases, there would be a strong economic motive for that individual to look for and find work.

Inevitably, the current income contribution of the discouraged worker is much more important to low-income than to high-income families (see Table 5.5). When individual income is subtracted from family income, the proportion of discouraged worker families with monthly incomes of $100 or less increases from 7 to 22 percent. Ninety-one percent of these households would have no income without the discouraged worker's contribution. On the other extreme, discouraged workers contribute a very modest share of family income to families with monthly incomes over $700.

Those families who depend wholly on the generally meager income of a discouraged worker are probably not doing well. Who are they? Analysis shows that they have these characteristics:

Table 5.5
Family Income (FI) Less Individual Income (II) for Discouraged and Unemployed Workers (as percentages)

Income ($)	Discouraged		Unemployed	
	Total	FI-II	Total	FI-II
0- 100	7.4	22.3	9.9	27.1
100- 300	7.2	3.9	9.4	5.0
300- 500	8.4	7.6	10.6	7.3
501- 700	8.3	5.2	9.6	7.4
701- 900	7.6	5.8	8.0	6.1
901-1,500	18.7	16.6	17.2	15.5
1,501-3,000	28.3	26.1	24.1	21.6
3,001+	14.0	12.6	11.4	10.1

Source: 1984 SIPP.

- Marital status: Forty percent are single, so that family income is simply personal income. Those who have worked in the past are twice (68 percent) as likely to be single as those with no work experience (34 percent). Fifty percent are widowed, divorced, or separated. Those with no work experience constitute 46 percent of the families wholly dependent on the discouraged worker's income, while those with work experience account for just 4 percent.

- Sex: The majority of the discouraged workers in these households (60 percent) are women, which is about the same proportion as that observed for the overall discouraged worker sample. Those with no work experience are twice as likely (66 percent) to be in households with no other source of income as those with work experience (31 percent).

- Education: Forty-one percent of these discouraged workers are high school dropouts.

- Age: Twenty-four percent are 60 years of age or older.

Demographically, families of discouraged workers with higher incomes are very different from those with no income:

- Marital status: Those with higher income are more likely to be single (71 percent versus 40 percent).

- Race: They are less likely to be black (13 percent versus 25 percent).

- Age: They are less likely to be nearing retirement age, that is, 60 years of age or older (4 percent versus 24 percent).

However, higher- and lower-income discouraged workers are similar in terms of sex and education.

Table 5.6

Family Income Source of Discouraged and Unemployed Workers by Family Size

Income Source:	******1***** Disc	Unem	******2***** Disc	Unem	****3-4***** Disc	Unem	*****5+***** Disc	Unem
SS + Wage	0.0	0.0	8.5	4.1	8.4	8.2	10.9	9.4
SS	44.7	11.9	20.5	13.3	6.3	6.9	3.9	4.2
AFDC	0.0	1.3	7.8	6.4	9.6	9.1	13.0	10.5
Wage only	13.7	0.0	44.8	50.5	66.5	60.9	57.4	55.3
Other	41.5	86.8	17.3	25.7	6.4	14.9	0.8	20.6

Source: 1984 SIPP.

Table 5.7

Family Incomes of Discouraged and Unemployed Workers by Family Size (as percentages)

Monthly Family Income:	******1***** Disc	Unem	******2***** Disc	Unem	****3-4***** Disc	Unem	*****5+***** Disc	Unem
0-100	31.7	44.2	6.9	11.3	3.6	5.6	2.7	1.3
101-300	19.8	23.4	11.3	10.2	5.8	7.5	0.8	5.4
301-500	16.1	14.8	12.8	16.0	8.4	8.8	2.4	8.4
501-700	17.2	11.0	10.5	10.2	6.1	8.3	6.8	15.0
701-900	9.0	3.1	9.3	9.1	8.3	7.6	5.2	9.8
901-1,500	6.4	2.7	20.3	18.5	16.9	19.8	23.7	18.3
1,501-3,000	1.0	0.8	24.7	19.3	34.6	30.2	33.8	29.9
3,001+	0.0	0.0	4.4	4.5	16.3	12.2	24.7	18.9

Source: 1984 SIPP.

Note: Line indicates poverty level.

Family Size

Analysis of the individual's and family's income and income sources provide a few pieces of the discouraged worker puzzle (see Table 5.3). The picture becomes clearer still when data on family size, income, and income sources are combined (see Tables 5.6, 5.7, and 5.8, respectively).

About one-half of single discouraged workers are either receiving Social Security or other pension benefits. Only 14 percent depend on wages for income. Nearly one-half (44.8 percent) of the two-member families rely on wage income, while another 29 percent depend on Social Security alone or plus wages. Only 8 percent of the couples rely on AFDC. Well over one-half of families with at

Table 5.8

Primary Income Sources of Discouraged and Unemployed Worker Families by Family Income

Income Ranges:	PRIMARY INCOME SOURCE				
	SS/Wage	SS	AFDC	Wage	All Other
$ 0-100					
Discouraged	0.0	0.0	0.0	22.4	77.6
Unemployed	0.0	0.0	1.3	8.8	89.9
$101-300					
Discouraged	0.0	6.9	39.1	9.3	44.7
Unemployed	0.0	5.9	33.0	10.3	50.9
$301-500					
Discouraged	0.0	26.3	23.2	15.3	35.0
Unemployed	0.0	15.4	21.0	12.5	51.0
$501-700					
Discouraged	3.3	27.5	20.7	32.7	15.8
Unemployed	3.2	11.8	14.5	37.6	32.9
$701-900					
Discouraged	7.8	27.0	5.4	44.5	15.3
Unemployed	3.4	11.2	11.1	49.3	25.5
$901-1,500					
Discouraged	11.1	14.0	8.6	52.8	9.7
Unemployed	10.3	10.6	2.0	61.5	15.5
$1,501-3,000					
Discouraged	13.4	7.3	1.3	73.9	4.0
Unemployed	14.0	4.3	0.4	76.4	5.0
$3,000+					
Discouraged	7.3	1.5	0.0	84.6	6.6
Unemployed	8.5	1.4	0.0	86.5	3.5

Source: 1984 SIPP.

Note: Row percentages total 100.0.

least three members rely primarily on earned income. Retirees comprise a much smaller proportion in this size range. The larger families also are slightly more likely than one- or two-person households to depend on AFDC.

Large families of unemployed workers resemble those of discouraged workers, in that their wage income usually exceeds their income from all other sources combined. However, unemployed families with five or more members are 20 times more likely than discouraged workers families of comparable size to receive "other income." A great deal of this difference is accounted for by the receipt of unemployment benefits by the unemployed.

Among discouraged workers, family size helps to determine whether the family's income places it above or below the federal poverty level (see Table 5.7). However, it is the single person rather than the large family who is most likely to be poor. Of the single discouraged workers, 68 percent have incomes below the poverty level,[6] whereas only 42 percent of families with two to four members, and 42 percent of those with at least five members are poor.[7]

Different *levels* of income are partly a reflection of different *sources* of income (see Table 5.8). Wages are the primary income source of just one-fourth of discouraged worker families in the lowest income category (earning $100 a month or less); above $500 a month, progressively more families rely on wages. Above $900 a month, wages are the primary income source of most discouraged worker families. The discouraged worker families that have higher-than-poverty-level incomes are mainly those with a working member. On the other hand, work does not always provide enough income to reach this level. Many members of discouraged worker families hold jobs offering only minimum wages, or work only part-time. Twenty-six percent of the discouraged worker population lost or quit part-time jobs over the past four months; most of those jobs provided very limited income gains.

Families receiving AFDC benefits cluster mostly in the income range from $101 to $700 monthly. Aid to Families with Dependent Children (AFDC) is the primary source of income for 21 to 39 percent of discouraged worker families in these income categories. This clustering reflects AFDC levels set for each family size, in each state's program.

Social Security beneficiaries are clustered as well, but at slightly higher income levels than AFDC recipients. Social Security is the major income source for about 27 percent of those with incomes ranging from $301 to $900 monthly.

"Other income" varies inversely with wages. Seventy-eight percent of those with monthly incomes of $100 or less rely on multiple sources. This percentage decreases consistently as one moves to higher income levels. Many of the poorer families or single people relying on other income are receiving small pensions and may work occasionally for wage income. A few take in boarders.

Noncash Benefits

Apart from government transfer payments (e.g., AFDC, SSI, or veterans' benefits), discouraged worker families may also receive government noncash benefits (U.S. General Accounting Office 1986a). Food stamps, health insurance (Medicaid and Medicare), school lunch programs, tuition for training for schooling, day care, and subsidized transportation are some of the major noncash benefits available to the poor. Some of these benefits, especially health insurance and food stamps, represent substantial savings to people who would otherwise have to provide for themselves or do without. For example, for a family of four in Ohio, privately purchased health insurance can cost as much as $3,000 annually.

To the extent that discouraged worker families obtain noncash benefits, then, their actual incomes will be higher (by including the cash value of noncash benefits) than they would be otherwise. The combined value of cash transfer payments and noncash benefits will be as high as or higher than, in some cases,

Table 5.9
Receipt of Noncash Benefits for Discouraged and Unemployed Workers (as percentages)

```
*****************************************************************************
Benefit:                             Discouraged                 Unemployed
-----------------------------------------------------------------------------

Some food stamps                        23.4                        26.0

Some benefit, but no
  food stamps                           12.8                        11.0

No non-cash benefit                     63.8                        63.0

Totals                                 100.0                       100.0

*****************************************************************************

Source:   1984 SIPP.
```

the equivalent income that the family could have obtained if the major bread-winner were working. In those cases, it may make no economic sense for a discouraged worker to reenter the labor force.

For a minority of both discouraged workers and the unemployed, noncash benefits are an important partial substitute for earnings and benefits that might be provided through work. About one-third (36 percent) of the discouraged worker population receive some noncash benefit (see Table 5.9). One-fourth receive food stamps, while only 13 percent receive some benefit other than food stamps. Most of those receiving noncash benefits are people on welfare. On the average, unemployed workers receive similar levels of support from noncash programs.

ECONOMIC INCENTIVE TO WORK

Would discouraged worker families be helped or harmed by finding a job, given that some of the family's unearned income—if any—would be reduced at the same time? If the federal poverty guideline is used as a base, 38 percent of the discouraged worker families are living at or below the official poverty line.[8] If discouraged worker income from all sources is subtracted from family income, the poverty rate increases to 47 percent.[9] In other words, the current contribution of discouraged workers to family income is relatively small in most cases. If discouraged workers were employed, on the other hand, this would dramatically reduce the proportion of these families living in poverty. If family income (not including present discouraged worker contributions) were supplemented by part-time work (20 hours a week) at the minimum wage, then the proportion of these households below the poverty level could drop to as low as 10 percent. If all discouraged workers were employed full-time (40 hours a week) at the minimum wage, possibly as few as 1 percent of the families would live at or below the official poverty line.

Table 5.10

Perspective on Family Debt One and Five Years Ago: Youngstown Discouraged and Unemployed (as percentages)

Compared to now, debt has:	DISCOURAGED		UNEMPLOYED	
	One Year	Five Years	One Year	Five Years
Increased	37.3	53.4	37.1	39.1
Remained the same	54.2	29.3	49.7	40.8
Decreased	8.5	17.2	12.6	19.5
Totals	100.0	100.0	100.0	100.0

Source: 1985 Youngstown Labor Force Follow-Up Survey.

This conclusion is based, however, on a "best-case" set of assumptions: it is assumed that earned income does not displace or disqualify the family for benefits received by other family members, and noncash benefits are ignored in the calculation of income. In reality, then, the calculation overstates the proportion of people who would be lifted out of poverty. Nevertheless, it suggests that modest earnings from low-wage jobs could have major positive effects.

COPING WITH JOBLESSNESS

The SIPP data provide a look at how much income discouraged workers receive from which sources. What the SIPP does not address is how discouraged workers view their own financial status or how they manage with reduced income. The Youngstown labor-force follow-up survey provides insights into how these households perceive and cope with their financial circumstances.

Discouraged and unemployed workers in the Youngstown metropolitan area were asked to assess their family debt now compared with one year and five years ago (see Table 5.10). Two-fifths of the discouraged workers in Youngstown had become increasingly indebted over the year prior to being interviewed. Nearly one-half were deeper in debt than they were five years earlier.

The unemployed indicated that they had experienced the same changes in debt levels as the discouraged over the past year. They were, however, less likely to have gone farther into debt over the five-year period. One explanation for this may be that the unemployed have been jobless for shorter periods than the discouraged. However, it also is likely that the larger proportion of people who have never worked in the discouraged worker group means that many have been worse off for longer periods than the unemployed.

Discouraged and unemployed workers were also asked about their overall financial situation in the past and in the future (see Table 5.11). The overall financial situation, including income, was rated *worse* at the present time than

Table 5.11
How the Jobless View Their Financial Situation: Youngstown Discouraged and Unemployed (as percentages)

Coping:	Discouraged	Unemployed
Financial situation now as compared to year ago		
Better now	21.3	25.9
Same	41.0	29.2
Worse now	31.1	43.2
Uncertain	6.6	1.6
Income now as compared to year ago		
More now	21.7	24.5
About same	48.3	39.1
Less now	30.0	36.4
Financial situation now as compared to five years ago		
Better now	35.1	31.5
Same	19.3	11.6
Worse now	40.4	55.2
Uncertain	5.3	1.7
Financial situation now compared to year from now		
Will be better	37.1	38.8
Same	45.2	39.9
Will be worse	6.5	6.6
Uncertain	11.3	14.8
Financial situation now compared to five years from now		
Will be better	61.7	62.0
Same	11.7	13.4
Will be worse	3.3	3.9
Uncertain	23.3	20.1
N	102	128

Source: 1985 Youngstown Labor Force Follow-up.

it was one and five years ago by about one-third of Youngstown's discouraged workers, but it was rated *better* by one-fourth. Many fewer of the discouraged than the unemployed perceived their financial situation to be worse than one and five years earlier.

Even though many discouraged and unemployed workers are poor, most are optimistic about their economic futures. Fewer than 10 percent believe that their short- and long-term financial prospects are worse than their present situation.

When asked to explain how their families made ends meet with jobless members having less income than in the past (see Table 5.12), most said that the

Table 5.12

Making Ends Meet: Youngstown Discouraged and Unemployed (percentage giving each answer)

```
************************************************************************
Activity*:                               Discouraged          Unemployed
------------------------------------------------------------------------


Borrow money from friends
  and relatives                             36.8                 36.9

Draw money from savings                     63.1                 51.5

Sell home                                    2.6                  1.0

Move back with relatives                     5.3                 12.6

Sell car                                    13.2                  8.7

Withdraw from school
  (child or self)                            2.6                  5.8

Give up vacation                            28.9                 41.7

Cut back on entertainment                    0.5                 64.0

Change dietary habits                       28.9                 21.4

N                                             76                  103

************************************************************************
Source:   1985 Youngstown Labor Force Follow-up Survey.

*Refers to actions over the past year.
```

family was forced to give up a great deal in the past year, just to get by. Two-thirds were forced to use savings. One-third had to borrow money from friends or relatives. Thirteen percent had to sell an automobile. A few had to sell homes and move in with relatives. Nearly one-fourth had changed their eating habits to reduce expenses.

CONCLUSION

Using the federal poverty standard as a benchmark, 62 percent of discouraged workers in the United States have enough family income so that there is no overpowering economic need for them to be employed. On the other hand, 38 percent, or 520,000 discouraged worker families, are in dire economic straits, which could be relieved by steady employment of the discouraged worker member.

Income, of course, is a fairly objective measure of need. To fully appreciate the situation of these marginal workers and their families, we also must look at their attitudes and motivation: the psychology of discouragement. How discouraged workers view life and work is the subject of the next chapter.

APPENDIX

Income is more complex to measure and confusing to interpret than might be expected. On the 1984 SIPP survey schedule, for example, respondents are asked to report income from dozens of sources for each of four months preceding the interview date. These figures are summed to yield four separate monthly income figures. Respondents must recall income by month and by income source. Additionally, since some respondents are surrogates, that is, responding on behalf of family members who are absent, respondents must have detailed knowledge of income of other members.

Confusion enters in terms of deciding how to represent and interpret individual income. A respondent may have no income during the four-month reference period, but may have had income before and after. Using the four months to calculate an estimated average annual income would, therefore, be highly misleading. If a respondent had a high income in any month, average annual income estimates could be distorted as well.

In this study, analyses were conducted initially on the first month of the four-month reference period. This seemed to make sense, in that labor-force statistics are monthly based, and a measure of a single month of income would constitute one point in time. During any given month, of course, a certain proportion of the labor force would have no income, while others would. Of those having income, some earned more, others less.

As a control for bias, the percentage of people who had income in one, two, three, or four months during the four-month reference period was calculated. This provides a more dynamic picture of income changes. It is no substitute, however, for income data on a monthly basis taken for an entire year.

Table 5.13 shows that about one-third (32 percent) of the discouraged and two-fifths (42 percent) of the unemployed had no income in any of the four months. By contrast, nearly one-half of the sample had income in all four referenced months.

Table 5.13 also shows that, for discouraged and unemployed workers alike, the first reference month yields the highest number of people with income and that, for each successive month, fewer and fewer people report income. However, there is only a five percentage point difference between the initial month and the fourth month. This pattern suggests that results would be similar in the aggregate, regardless of the reference month picked for analysis.

Next, the number of months with income and the amount of income for each month (the two variables above) were cross-tabulated for both the discouraged and unemployed. Thus, it was possible to see whether groups with different monthly income receipts were unevenly distributed in each of the four reference months. If they were very unevenly distributed, then using any given reference month would lead to biases. Results showed that groups were evenly distributed so that bias was not in evidence.

We looked at income sources for each month in the reference period at the

Table 5.13

Analysis of Possible Bias in Monthly Reported Income Figures (as percentages)

```
*******************************************************************
                                        Discouraged      Unemployed
-------------------------------------------------------------------

Number of months in reference period received income:
-------------------------------------------------------------------

                    0                     32.2             41.5
                    1                      7.6              5.8
                    2                      7.1              3.4
                    3                      5.1              2.7
                    4                     48.0             46.6

-------------------------------------------------------------------
Received income in reference months, 1,2,3, and 4, respectively:
-------------------------------------------------------------------

                    1                     60.1             55.1
                    2                     57.6             51.4
                    3                     56.2             50.5
                    4                     55.1             50.3

*******************************************************************

Source:  1984 SIPP.
```

aggregate level for discouraged and unemployed workers. Percentages from each income source remained nearly identical for both groups. For example, Social Security recipients varied between 34.5 to 33.8 percent, and those receiving AFDC between 11.2 and 10.8 percent for the discouraged and unemployed, respectively. Again, this added support to our contention that using any given reference month introduces little bias.

Were monthly income figures to be available for an entire year, problems in interpretation would continue to exist. Respondents in the study are interviewed in "waves," that is, at different times during the year, so that the four-month reference period is not the same for everyone in the sample. This design feature of the sample, however, provides a more reliable picture of incomes for any given month in the aggregate.

NOTES

1. See Appendix for detailed methodological explanation and analysis.

2. Personal income may be understated because of earnings in the "hidden economy": doing odd jobs for cash, engaging in illegal activity (e.g., drugs, gambling, or prostitution), or obtaining financial help from friends or relatives.

3. In order to simplify the analysis, we focus on the family rather than the household. Family refers to related members living together, while household includes related an unrelated people living together.

4. Family income is subject to the same limitations as individual income, as described in note 2.

5. Ten percent of the discouraged worker population identified by the CPS was living outside a family. The discrepancy probably results from differences in sample weightings, time frame for the study, and sampling error.

6. Family definitions are based on 1984 poverty income guidelines as published in the following: U.S. Bureau of the Census, "Characteristics of the Population Below Poverty Level, 1984," P60–152 (Washington, D.C.: Government Printing Office, 1986), p. 122.

7. An identical relationship between family size and income was observed for unemployed workers, although in every case, the proportion of unemployed people falling below the poverty level exceeded that of the discouraged group.

8. Based on family income for the first reference month (of four) on the 1984 SIPP survey.

9. Family and discouraged worker incomes include all cash income sources, but not noncash benefits. In some cases, discouraged workers might have had earned income as well because of a recent layoff, although this would be rare.

6 *VIEWING LIFE AND WORK*

Some people look at work as a necessary means to other things they need or value. Some make it a central part of their identity, a psychological necessity. Yet to some, work is not so important. The need to work is not so keenly felt; other demands on time and energy, and other sources of identity and meaning outweigh the attraction of paid employment.

The sometimes devastating psychological effect of job loss reflects the central place that paid work holds in the lives of many Americans. Others would share the more ambivalent and ironic view that Jerome K. Jerome expressed 100 years ago: "I like work: it fascinates me. I can sit down and look at it for hours. I love to keep it by me: the idea of getting rid of it nearly breaks my heart."

Yet, even for those less infatuated with it, work serves multiple functions: it is a source of income, fulfills a need to be active, structures time for most of the day, promotes creativity and mastery, offers companionship, and instills a sense of purpose (Hayes and Nutman 1981).

Not everyone wants to or needs to work for wages. For some, work is unpleasant, even intolerable.[1] People who have home-management responsibilities may work hard but do not depend on wages from the marketplace; nor do they receive the nonmonetary rewards (or penalties) of work in an environment of competition and formal organizations. Those who can rely on the resources of others need not bother with the labor market. A minority of the homeless could be said to have turned joblessness into a lifestyle (Redburn and Buss 1986). For people who are not emotionally attached to work and who do not need work, nonparticipation—far from being a traumatic event—may not be particularly unsettling.

If most discouraged workers are disappointed and frustrated because they want jobs, then being without work should produce, for them, the same kind of distress experienced by the unemployed. However, if discouraged workers are more like other groups not in the labor force, who *say* they do not want work, then they should be better adjusted to their lack of employment and show fewer symptoms of distress than the unemployed.

This chapter looks at the psychological status and attitudes of discouraged workers, in order to generate answers to three questions:

1. Are the psychological impacts of job loss common among the unemployed also apparent in the discouraged worker population?
2. Does their psychological status reveal anything about the likelihood that discouraged workers will return to the labor force?
3. Are there systematic differences in psychological status among discouraged workers?

For this analysis, data were drawn from the Youngstown–Warren CPS Follow-up Survey (Summer of 1985), in which 600 workers were interviewed, including 102 who are classified as discouraged.

To look at the psychology of discouragement, we have selected what we believe is the most applicable and revealing conceptualization of mental health or illness.

PSYCHOLOGICAL WELL-BEING CONCEPTUALIZED

Mental health or illness has been traditionally conceptualized in one of two ways. A medical model focuses on mental *illness*: the presence of observable or imputed signs or symptoms that mental health professionals believe are indicative of disease (Cassimatis 1979). Mental health, then, is defined negatively, as the absence of disease. Physical health, which is defined as the absence of corporeal illness or disease, provides an analog for this model of mental health.

A competing sociopsychological model of mental health does not focus on the identification of psychopathological symptoms, but instead on the problems that all people contend with—the stresses and strains of everyday life (see Bradburn 1969; Warr 1978). Mental health is understood as a general sense of well-being in which a person has both positive (i.e., related to happiness, job satisfaction, and self-esteem) and negative (i.e., related to worry, unhappiness, and dissatisfaction) states. Positive and negative states for individuals, importantly, are not represented as polar opposites on a single continuum. Positive and negative states can and do exist independently from one another. For example, a person may be happy with life generally (a positive state) while being distressed over problems on the job (a negative state). Overall mental health is a function of the extent to which a person achieves positive and eliminates negative states.

Figure 6.1
The Structure of Psychological Well-Being

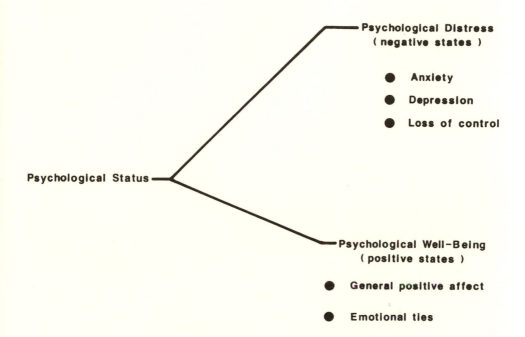

The model is not "psychopathology seeking," but instead attempts to separate those persons who are successfully coping from those who are not.

One advantage of the sociopsychological model for analysis of discouraged or unemployed workers is the ability it gives us to measure *both* negative and positive reactions to lack of work.

Psychological well-being has been measured in many ways (see Health Resources Administration 1977; Warr and Wall 1975). For this analysis, the Mental Health Inventory (MHI), developed by the Rand Corporation, was selected.[2]

Mental health thus is treated as having two broad components: psychological well-being (positive states) and psychological distress (negative states) (see Figure 6.1). Well-being is composed of two scales or indices: general positive affect, based on 11 items; and emotional ties, having two items. Distress encompasses three scales: anxiety, with nine items; depression, with 41; and loss of behavioral–emotional control, with nine.[3]

THE PSYCHOLOGY OF DISCOURAGEMENT

Confirming what others have found, the Youngstown area survey results show that psychological status is related to employment status, but the relationship is more complex than generally appreciated. Discouraged workers have a psychological profile that distinguishes them from other groups in and outside the labor force.

Those who are employed full-time, on the average, are the least distressed labor-force group and have a better sense of well-being than any other (see Figures 6.2a and b). The unemployed worker, in contrast, is the most distressed and has the lowest sense of well-being. This finding is consistent with the notion that, *ceteris paribus*, full-time work is a positive influence on mental health, while unemployment has just the opposite effect.

Discouraged workers, on the average, score between the extremes of the full-time employed and unemployed, manifesting more positive states on both the psychological distress and well-being measures than the unemployed.

Discouraged workers resemble two other groups in the labor force more closely than they do the unemployed: the working poor and employed part-time workers seeking full-time work. This is consistent with the evidence that discouraged workers—although not themselves in the labor force—typically come from poor families or are poor themselves.

Not only did all of the preceding comparisons hold true for two composite indices, psychological distress and well-being, but they also showed consistency across the individual scales (with the exception of emotional ties) making up each index (see Table 6.1). Discouraged workers scored consistently between the employed and unemployed on measures of anxiety, depression, loss of control, and positive affect.

Because positive and negative psychological states can coexist, it is important to look at the group scores on both psychological dimensions: distress and well-being. When the groups' average scores were arrayed on both dimensions, their relative psychological states became readily apparent (see Figure 6.3). Those strongly attached to the labor force express negative psychological states—either more distress or less well-being—when they are not working and desire jobs or are working at low-pay–low status jobs. On the average, those actively seeking work (the unemployed) show the most distress and the lowest sense of well-being.

Workers forced to retire early, like discouraged workers, are people who have been involuntarily excluded from the labor force. We hypothesized, therefore, that they would have a similar psychological profile. However, in their pattern of emotional states, the forceably retired are more like the full-time employed than like the discouraged (see Figure 6.3). Those forced to retire, on the average, appear to have more positive mental health than the discouraged. This could mean that, although the initial or even anticipated shock of job loss and retirement may produce short-term distress, over the longer term the forceably retired often adjust to their new circumstances. By definition, on the other hand, the discouraged continue to express dissatisfaction over being out of the work force.

Those employed in good jobs or who have resources though forced to retire more often report positive psychological states. In between, along with the working poor, stand the discouraged.

Figure 6.2a
Psychological Status by Selected Labor Force Categories, Psychological Distress

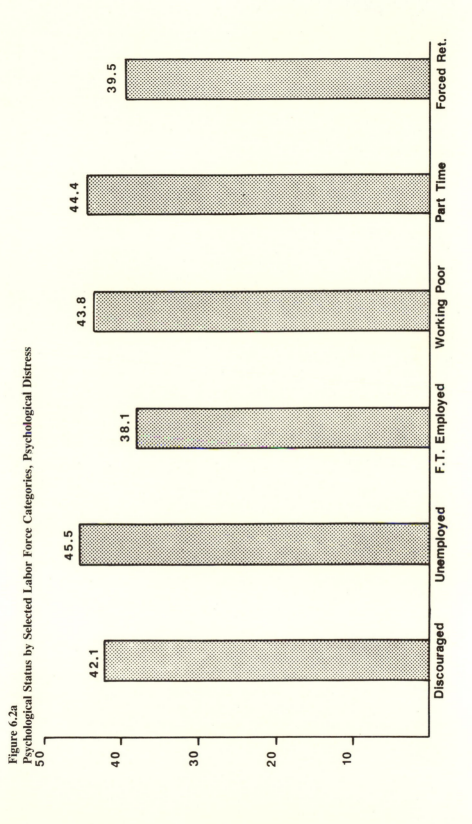

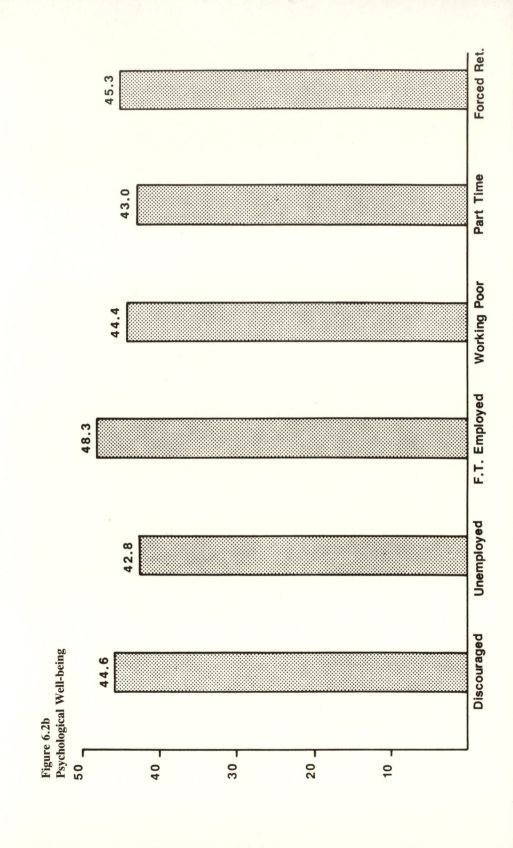

Figure 6.2b
Psychological Well-being

Table 6.1
Psychological Status by Selected Labor-Force Categories

Scales:	Official Disc.	Official Unemp.	Full-time Employed	Working Poor	Part-time	Forced Retired	F ratio	Stat. Sign.
Psychological Distress	42.1	45.5	38.1	43.8	44.4	39.5	5.055	.000
Anxiety	19.4	20.9	18.0	19.8	21.5	18.4	3.980	.002
Depression	9.2	9.5	7.6	9.1	8.9	7.8	6.351	.000
Loss of control	13.5	15.1	12.4	15.0	14.0	13.3	4.609	.000
Psychological Well-being	44.6	42.8	48.3	44.4	43.0	45.3	5.106	.000
Positive affect	35.5	33.9	38.8	35.4	34.0	36.5	5.924	.000
Emotional ties	9.1	9.0	9.5	9.1	9.0	8.7	1.219	.299

Source: 1985 Youngstown Labor Force Follow-up Survey.

Note: Figures are average scores on psychological well-being measures.
        The higher the score, the greater well-being or distress, respectively.
        Analysis of variance was used to determine statistical significance.

Demographics

Within the group of discouraged workers, demographic characteristics were not good predictors of psychological status. As shown in Table 6.2, race was one measured characteristic that was associated with both the distress and well-being scales. Contrary to expectations, though, black discouraged workers were less distressed and scored higher on the well being index than did whites. This indicated that blacks in this group were more likely to have adjusted well to joblessness and attendant poverty. This finding, by itself, does not offer much insight. Unfortunately, the size of the sample is too small to allow a fuller exploration of the finding with this particular data set.

Among discouraged workers, age was associated with greater feelings of psychological well-being. Older workers (55 years and older) also showed lower levels of distress than those who were younger. Many of these older workers retired after a long work career and were not seriously interested in full-time work. Apparently, the older discouraged worker responded positively overall to his or her status outside the labor force.

Marital status was associated with psychological well-being and not with psychological distress. Discouraged workers who were married had a greater sense of well-being than those who had never been married or were widowed,

Figure 6.3
Spatial Profile of Labor-Force Mental Health

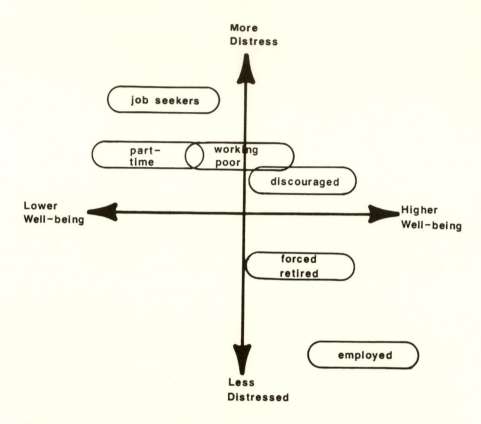

divorced, or separated. Similar findings have been reported in other contexts and may reflect the more supportive psychological environment that marriage offers, or the greater financial security of a household with a second potential breadwinner, and/or preexisting differences in the psychological status of married and unmarried people.

Among discouraged workers, income was not significantly associated with psychological status.

Effect of Time

The length of time since a person last worked is likely to affect his or her psychological status. On the average, people who were weakly attached to the labor force—those without work for long periods of time and those who had yet to hold down a job—reported a much more positive psychological status than those who were more recently unemployed and presumably more strongly attached to and more closely associated with the labor force (see Figure 6.4).

Table 6.2
Psychological Status for Discouraged Workers by Age, Race, Sex, Education, and Marital Status

Demographic:	N	Psychological Distress Mean	F ratio	Sign.	Psychological Well-Being Mean	F ratio	Sign.
Age							
16-24 years	25	47.9			43.6		
25-54 years	30	45.1	3.591	.032	42.8	0.923	.401
55+ years	27	38.1			45.9		
Race							
white	71	44.2	6.941	.010	43.3	4.751	..032
other	30	37.2			47.5		
Sex							
male	40	40.3	1.339	.250	46.5	2.932	.090
female	61	43.3			43.4		
Education							
– high school	38	42.5	0.000	.992	42.9	2.040	.157
+ high school	58	42.5			45.6		
Marital Status							
never married	38	42.5			43.0		
now married	48	40.6	1.050	.354	47.0	3.768	.027
others	14	46.0			40.8		

Source: 1985 Youngstown Labor Force Follow-up Survey.

Note: See note for Table 6.1.

The pattern suggests that once a worker gave up looking for work, or once he or she had been out of (or never in) the labor force for a time, psychological status improved. The further a person stood from recent work experience, the more he or she appeared to become complacent about circumstances and the less likely to initiate activities to change the situation.

When the length of time since the individual last worked was compared with psychological status among discouraged workers only, the strong association noted for all adults disappeared[4]; that is, psychological distress and well-being were not related to length of time out of work. This is a surprising and potentially important result. If complacency does not grow with length of time out of the labor force for those who continue to express discouragement, unlike other unemployed workers, then those out of work for long periods may respond as well to reemployment opportunities as those just recently unemployed.

CONCLUSION

If those once strongly attached to the labor force become weakly attached, they become more difficult to place in jobs. A person who has adjusted to life without work may never return to the stress and challenge of the labor market,

Figure 6.4
Time Component in Mental Health

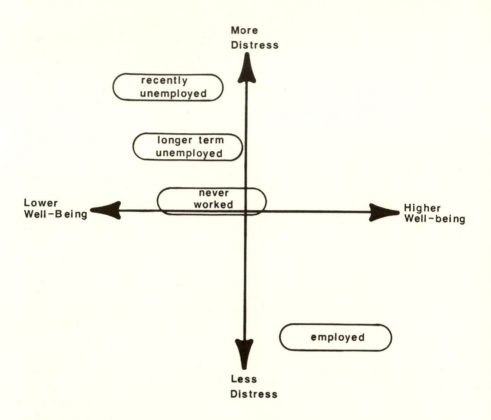

especially if this means working at a low-status, low-paying job. This has implications for public policy.

In the first place, early interventions that forestall this process of detachment may prove cost-effective. In the second place, programs aimed at those least attached to work, including those who have never worked, must make work seem to be an attractive option before they can hope to succeed.

In a world of scarce public resources, discouraged workers may constitute a target of opportunity for programs to prepare people for productive employment. Although, as a group, they express relatively strong feelings of well-being, many also continue to express distress at not working.

Other studies (e.g., Finegan 1978) have found that discouraged workers often will not take jobs when offered; that many have unrealistic requirements for accepting jobs (e.g., high salary coupled with low skill levels and protracted work days and hours); and that they often are unskilled and lack experience, are perhaps difficult to train, and frequently have other problems (such as criminal records, child-rearing responsibilities, or disabilities) that block them from working. Perhaps, therefore, resources would be better invested in improving the quality of life and security of the working poor and part-time employed: two groups who have a more clearly demonstrated attachment to the work force. To better judge the potential employability of discouraged workers, we need to take a closer look at specific characteristics that may make it difficult for them to find or keep good jobs.

NOTES

1. Garraty (1978) has reviewed the history of the ideas of employment and leisure.

2. The MHI represents an advancement over other instruments used in this line of inquiry (Veit and Ware 1983; Ware et al. 1979).

3. Measures of well-being and distress may be combined in the overall index of mental health. We have elected not to focus analysis at this abstract level, but instead have concentrated on individual measures of well-being and distress. Detailed analyses of the mathematical properties of the scales can be found in Veit and Ware (1983).

4. Because no statistically significant differences were observed, tabular data were not reported.

7   *SEEKING WORK*

Although three out of four discouraged workers say they intend to look for work in the future, the evidence that they will follow through is fairly weak. Fully one-half have made no effort to find a job for at least a year. Only two-fifths of those who actually found jobs still held them one year later, perhaps a further indication of low motivation (Job 1979; Flaim 1984; Finegan 1978). Earlier researchers have concluded from their observations that the discouraged worker population is weakly attached to the labor force.

Although strong circumstantial evidence suggests that many discouraged workers are less than eager to work, previous researchers have not had direct information about discouraged workers' preparation for work, their employment expectations, and job-search strategy. In this chapter, such additional evidence is brought to bear on one of the central unanswered questions about discouraged workers: what keeps them from looking for and finding work?

Before answering this broader question, a series of more specific ones regarding *preparation* for and *motivation* to work must be answered.

1. How qualified are discouraged workers for work, as measured by their education, job skills, and previous work experience?
2. How likely are they to have participated in retraining or education programs to improve their employability?
3. How stable has their past employment experience been?

Concerning their motivation to work:

4. What kinds of jobs are discouraged workers seeking? How many hours per week do they expect to work? What are their salary requirements? What employment benefits do they desire?

5. When was the last time work was sought? When work was last sought, how was the job search executed? Are discouraged workers likely to move long distances in search of work?

6. If they intend to seek work in the future, how likely is it that they will accept the kinds of jobs that will most likely be offered to them?

7. How likely are discouraged workers to become self-employed, as an alternative to working for others?

Two Youngstown area surveys—the Local CPS Follow-up Survey, from the summer of 1985, and the Discouraged Worker Survey, conducted during the fall of 1985—help to answer these questions. Data from the CPS and SIPP data sets are used, where possible, to provide a national perspective.

PREPARATION FOR WORK

The education, job-skills training, and past job experience of discouraged workers will largely determine their employment prospects. From the standpoint of public policy, it would be useful to know whether a lack of schooling, job-related skills, or credentials are major barriers to their going to work, and to what extent they limit the range of jobs discouraged workers may reasonably expect to hold.

If discouraged workers are, by and large, less qualified for work, by these fairly objective measures, than those with whom they must compete—the unemployed—then this may explain why they have taken themselves out of the labor market. If they resemble the unemployed in their apparent qualifications, then we must still ask what it would take for either group to compete more successfully for jobs.

Education and Skills

Most discouraged workers believe that the jobs they previously held required very little formal education and even less specialized training. One-third of the jobs previously held by the discouraged required no formal education (see Table 7.1). Many of these jobs involved manual labor. Only 15 percent required a college degree. College-level jobs were primarily in management. The remaining one-half of the jobs held appeared to require a high school or vocational diploma.

More than one-half of the discouraged previously held jobs they perceived as requiring little or no training: about one in ten required no training, while two-fifths needed less than a month of training.[1]

Although some discouraged workers who have never worked may have been

Table 7.1

Qualifications for Last Job: Youngstown Discouraged, Unemployed, and Employed

Indicator:	Discouraged	Unemployed	Employed
Formal education to get the kind of job you had?			
No formal education	34.0	33.5	24.0
High school diploma	39.6	44.3	43.5
Tech school	11.3	14.2	14.2
College	15.1	6.3	13.7
Graduate school	0.0	1.7	4.6
Totals	100.0	100.0	100.0
Amount of training on the job to handle your job?			
None	17.0	12.1	9.4
1 day but less than 1 month	37.7	44.8	30.8
1 month but less than 3 months	20.8	15.5	15.7
3 months but less than 1 year	9.4	9.2	13.1
1 year+	15.1	18.4	31.1
Totals	100.0	100.0	100.0

Source: 1985 Youngstown Labor Force Follow-up Survey.

involved in education and training programs related to specific jobs, the overall lack of preparation and work experience among the discouraged and unemployed generally suggests that these workers would be even less competitive with no work experience. At the very least, others can draw on some work experience, no matter how modest.

Lack of skills among the discouraged could be a major factor in explaining difficulties in employment. It should be noted that discouraged workers are no worse off in this respect than are the unemployed (see Table 7.1). However, when both groups are compared with those now holding jobs, the education and skills disadvantage of both groups, relative to the employed, becomes apparent. One-third of both the unemployed and discouraged previously held jobs requiring no formal education, compared with only one-fourth (24 percent) of the employed. While nearly one-third (31 percent) of the employed had participated in job-related training lasting at least a year, less than one-fifth of the unemployed and less than one-sixth of the discouraged workers had done so.

For the discouraged worker, then, a general lack of distress over being out of work (see chapter 6) may combine with uncompetitive skill levels to pose major barriers to labor-force participation. In this sense, many of the discouraged must be considered unlikely candidates for mainstream employment, but there are wide variations within the group.

Training and Plant Closings

Although most discouraged workers lack training, it may or may not follow that training programs are a help to them in gaining employment. The emphasis on retraining that follows many plant closings provides an opportunity to test the relationship between retraining and reemployment. When a plant closes, federal, state, and local officials are likely to descend on displaced workers with a smorgasbord of training options (see Buss and Vaughan 1988). This provides a chance to measure both the level of laid-off workers' interest in seeking reemployment through retraining and the effectiveness of retraining in helping them obtain new jobs. As far as the discouraged worker is concerned, the opportunity to participate in retraining will never be better. Yet, will the retraining attract discouraged workers and will it lead to jobs?

Nationally, 15 percent of the workers involved in a plant closing participated in a training program between 1982 and 1984. Of those participating in any training, ranging from very limited job preparation (e.g., résumé preparation) to more career-oriented classroom work and on-the-job training (OJT), about 75 percent were subsequently reemployed.[2]

Among steelworkers in Youngstown, participation rates were similar to the national figures, at 20 percent, but Youngstown workers had markedly less success at reemployment: only 37 percent obtained jobs—about half the national success rate. This difference is probably at least partly due to a relative lack of employment opportunities in an area suffering a series of massive layoffs in the manufacturing sector.

Although few workers who are eligible participate in training, those who do are able to find jobs.

Of the unemployed workers surveyed with the Training Supplement to the national plant-closing Current Population Survey (CPS), 13 percent participated in training programs.[3] However, in a startling contrast, *none* of the discouraged workers surveyed took training.

Because both discouraged and unemployed workers participate in training programs at such low rates, both nationally and locally, training does not by itself explain why one group has given up looking for work, while the other persists in searching for a job.

Those low participation rates suggest that training had not been perceived by either group as being a promising path to reemployment. One good possibility is that lack of training participation has contributed to their lack of success in finding or holding jobs. Although our knowledge is incomplete, it appears from some local studies (e.g., Buss and Redburn 1983) that workers do not participate for at least four reasons:

- Training is perceived as leading to low-paying or entry-level positions.

- A stigma is associated with returning to the classroom, especially among those who did not do well in school and for those who have been out of school for a long time.

• Training is viewed as a waste of time because it often does not lead to a job.

• Finally, some workers are reluctant to forgo wages for any length of time in favor of a risky venture like retraining.

Job Stability

Some unemployed and discouraged workers interviewed in the 1984 National CPS Plant Closing Supplement, had a history of unstable employment over the preceding ten years (see Table 7.2). One-third of the discouraged held at least two jobs. Twenty-five percent received unemployment insurance benefits at least once. Twenty-two percent quit or lost at least two jobs, and one-fourth reported changing occupations. Another one-fourth were stably out of work, having held no job during the past decade.

Those work histories could have two alternative interpretations. Job change may indicate that discouraged workers really are attached to the labor force; they try to hold onto jobs but often cannot. Alternatively, job change, especially in low-wage, low-skill jobs may indicate limited motivation to work. Discouraged workers may only work when it is absolutely necessary or when they are in the mood. Of the two possible explanations, the latter seems to fit better with other information. The unemployed continue to search for work after losing jobs. The less frequent job changes of the discouraged suggests that, on the average, they take longer to seek or find work after losing jobs. This could mean either that discouraged workers are less strongly oriented toward work than the unemployed or that they face greater barriers to successful job search. Next, we look more directly at the question of motivation.

EXPECTATIONS AND MOTIVATION

If discouraged workers have a limited desire to work or restrictive conditions on the jobs they will accept, then apart from their actual job qualifications, these attitudes may limit their prospects of finding the types of jobs they prefer. In this section, the 1984 national plant-closing supplement and 1985 Discouraged Workers Surveys are examined for insights on expectations and motivation.

Expressed Intention to Work

By their own testimony, most discouraged workers are willing to work. Nationally, 85 percent expressed an interest in getting a job when interviewed. Similarly, three-fourths of the discouraged workers in Youngstown indicated that they definitely wanted a job. However, the other one-fourth responded with a much more tentative "maybe."

Kinds of Jobs Preferred

More interesting than a general expression of a desire to work are the stated preferences of discouraged workers for particular types of jobs. Perhaps most startling is that 70 percent are not able to say what kinds of work they prefer. This suggests a lack of motivation or focus on finding a career. At least in the Youngstown area, the lion's share of those who do express preferences are not looking for executive, managerial, or professional positions. This group is at least realistic about their own levels of education and experience and what is required for highly skilled, high-paying positions.

It is also surprising that a majority of discouraged workers in Youngstown are not interested in full-time employment. More than one-half (57 percent) want part-time work. Only 28 percent would accept full-time work only. The remaining 15 percent would be willing to take either a full- or part-time job. Nationally, one-fourth of the discouraged workers are oriented more toward the secondary labor market: part-time, temporary, seasonal, benefitless, unskilled jobs. Workers demand less from those jobs, but also give less and get less.

Probably because so many prefer part-time to full-time work, discouraged workers also expect to work less than a 40-hour week: two-thirds wished to work 30 hours a week or less. Three-fourths would accept $200 or less a week in wages, equivalent to $10,400 annually. Discouraged worker expectations about work and compensation are consistent with what is available in the secondary labor market.

Few discouraged workers are so desperate that they will take any job offered. Their preferences for day- and night-shift work are illustrative. Most discouraged workers (60 percent) prefer the day shift, but many (39 percent) are willing to accept day- or night-shift work. Only a handful prefer the night shift. One possible reason why a large minority of discouraged workers do not dread the night shift is that, as part-time workers, they would not be required to spend a full shift away from home.

Job Prospects

By one important measure of expectations, the Youngstown discouraged workers really do sound discouraged. An overwhelming majority are dubious about ever obtaining a job like the one they lost (see Table 7.4). Almost 90 percent rate their chances as only "poor" to "fair." However, an identical proportion of the unemployed are similarly pessimistic, again casting doubt on the distinctiveness of discouraged workers and the meaning of the "discouraged" label. That widespread pessimism may well be a result of the massive losses in high-wage blue-collar industries in the Youngstown area over the past decade.

In the minds of most discouraged and unemployed workers, a new job probably means changing to a new or different occupation, something that is not easily accomplished by most people. Yet, what distinguishes those people who expect

Table 7.2
Ten-Year Work History (since 1974): Youngstown Discouraged and Unemployed
(as percentages)

```
**********************************************************
```

Item:	Discouraged	Unemployed
Number of employers		
0	25.4	5.9
1	42.9	36.0
2	14.3	26.3
3	6.3	13.4
4	3.2	10.8
5	3.2	2.7
6+	4.7	4.9
Number of times on U.I.		
0	75.0	53.3
1	18.3	25.5
2	1.7	9.8
3	0.0	4.9
4	1.7	3.3
5	0.0	0.5
6+	3.3	2.7
Number of jobs quit or lost		
0	45.0	26.5
1	33.3	35.1
2	10.0	20.0
3	5.0	10.8
4	1.7	3.8
5	1.7	1.1
6+	3.3	2.7
Changed occupations		
Yes	23.9	31.4
Number of times held more than one job		
0	85.7	86.0
1	3.6	8.7
2	1.8	2.3
3+	8.9	3.0
N	(102)	(128)

```
**********************************************************
```

Source: 1985 Youngstown Labor Force Follow-up Survey.

Table 7.3
Job Preferences among Discouraged Workers

```
**************************************************
Item:                                    %
--------------------------------------------------
Want a job now?
     Yes                                73.5
     Maybe                              26.5

Type of job wanted?
     Executive                           1.5
     Professional                        1.5
     Sales                               2.9
     Admin Support                      10.3
     Personal service                   2.9
     Other service                      5.9
     Precision prod                     4.4
     Oper fab, laborer                  1.5
     Don't know                        69.1

Full-time?
     Full-time                         27.7
     Part-time                         56.9
     Either                            15.4
Hours per week to work?
     1  -  5                            1.5
     6  - 10                            4.6
    11  - 15                            9.2
    16  - 20                           29.2
    21  - 30                           20.0
    31  - 40                           35.4

Salary requirements?   (weekly)
     §100                              51.7
     101-200                           26.7
     201-300                           10.0
     301-400                            5.0
     401-500                            5.0
     501-1000                           0.0
     1000+                              1.7

Shift requirements?
     day                               59.4
     night                              1.6
     either                            39.1
**************************************************
```

Source: Fall 1985 Discouraged Worker Survey.

Table 7.4
Job Prospects and Job Search: Youngstown Discouraged and Unemployed (as percentages)

Question:		Discouraged	Unemployed
Chances of finding	Excellent	6.9	4.7
job like one lost?	Good	6.9	9.4
	Fair	34.5	30.2
	Poor	51.7	55.7
Discouraged now	Very	23.7	42.5
about finding a	Somewhat	34.2	30.1
regular job soon?	A little	15.8	11.5
	Not at all	26.3	15.9
Number of months	0	68.0	78.3
willing to hold	1	12.0	3.3
out before taking	2	8.0	4.3
a job?	3	4.0	3.3
	4	0.0	2.2
	5	0.0	0.0
	6	4.0	4.3
	7-12	4.0	2.2
	12+	0.0	2.2
How important are	Very	44.1	30.4
your family and	Somewhat	29.4	38.3
friends in search-	Hardly at all	5.9	12.2
ing for jobs?	Not at all	20.6	19.1
Most important	Public employment agency	15.6	20.0
sources of job	Private employment agency	6.3	11.5
information?	Employer directly	40.6	33.0
	Friends and relatives	27.3	25.2
	Newspaper ads	12.1	10.4
How often examined	Never	63.9	44.4
out-of-town	Once or twice	16.7	34.2
newspapers.	Many times	19.4	21.4
Newspapers list jobs	Usually	3.3	10.9
for which you are	Sometimes	43.3	56.4
qualified?	Never	53.3	32.7
Considered moving	Yes, for employment reasons	50.0	50.0
from Youngstown in			
last five years?			
N		102	128

Source: 1985 Youngstown Labor Market Follow-up Survey.

111

to get a job similar to the one they lost from those who do not? The Youngstown studies do not include enough cases to conduct an extensive analysis. However, interviews with some discouraged workers suggest that many have unrealistic expectations about the labor market. For instance, many displaced steelworkers had trouble adjusting to the demise of steelmaking in Youngstown. They tended to believe, or were led to believe, that although steel jobs were not now available, eventually some scheme by the government, unions, or management would bring back the industry (Redburn and Buss 1984). Eight years later, not only had the jobs failed to return but also virtually all of the shutdown steel works had been demolished. Only then did some workers realize that they would never again work in the industry.

Perceived Job Chances. Discouragement is a label assigned to a person based on answers to selected Bureau of Labor Statistics (BLS) questions. Do these workers see themselves as discouraged, as the word is used in ordinary discussion? Over one-half (58 percent) of the officially discouraged think of themselves as either "very" or "somewhat" discouraged about finding work. On the other hand, nearly one-fourth are not discouraged at all. Ironically, though, *unemployed workers are more likely than the discouraged to be discouraged about finding a job*, with three-fourths describing themselves as either "very" or "somewhat" discouraged. Only 16 percent of the unemployed are "not at all" discouraged. This is a strange reversal, directly opposed to standard terminology and thinking about the relative positions of unemployed and discouraged workers.

If the unemployed are more often discouraged than the officially discouraged workers, and if a substantial minority of the officially discouraged do not think of themselves as discouraged, it is reasonable to conclude that the BLS definition of discouragement obfuscates rather than clarifies the situation. One reason why the controversy about discouraged workers persists is that neither side in the debate understands the other's interpretation of discouragement. The term discouragement is a case of technical language gone haywire, a point to which we will return in the final chapters.

Response to Job Offers. Perhaps the most stringent test of attachment to the labor force is the extent to which workers are offered jobs but turn them down. Only a handful of the Youngstown area discouraged (10 percent) and unemployed (12 percent) was offered jobs but rejected them. Those who turned down jobs did so for reasons usually involving wages, benefits, and quality of work life. While these percentages may seem low, we do not know what proportion of each group were offered jobs and accepted them during the same time period.

Economic necessity may only allow workers to be selective in reemployment until personal resources are depleted up to some limit. Those who were out of work in Youngstown expected to reach that limit fairly soon after being interviewed. The vast majority—both among the discouraged (80 percent) and among the unemployed (82 percent)—was unwilling to hold out more than one more month before taking a job. A small percentage (four to eight) was willing to wait indefinitely for the right job.

Even though most jobless people need to work and cannot hold out for long periods of time before reentering the labor force, some displaced workers in Youngstown have refused to accept jobs that are available because these jobs are not as good as the ones they have lost. The Youngstown research identified many former steelworkers—once the highest-paid group of blue-collar workers— who could not bring themselves to work for less than the old wage. About 22 percent of those who were laid off were in this category (Buss and Redburn 1987). Almost all of these placed the burden of earning income on their spouses. Although BLS surveys probably identify these workers as discouraged, in reality they are voluntarily out of the labor force.

Job Information Sources. Informal networks of relatives and acquaintances, often spread out across a community, can efficiently keep tabs and report on available jobs (see Buss and Redburn 1983). In Youngstown, family and friends were viewed by at least two-thirds of the discouraged and unemployed to be important in finding jobs. However, one-fifth indicated that they were no help at all. The informal network is of less help to the jobless when their skills are just not in demand or the worker has characteristics that make him or her difficult to place, for example, is older, disabled, alcoholic, criminal, or difficult to work with.

Published job listings are not widely used by the jobless to find work. Only one-fifth of the discouraged and unemployed workers in Youngstown searched for jobs using out-of-town newspapers. Perhaps one reason the unemployed and discouraged do not rely heavily on newspapers for their job search is that those in both groups rarely or never see job listings for which they are qualified.

As elaborated in the next section, workers are reluctant to leave their home communities; therefore, many feel no need to examine out-of-town newspapers. Those who do look at out-of-town newspapers apparently take the initiative seriously; in Youngstown, displaced workers could find these newspapers only at the main public library or state university library, which required considerable time and effort. Competition for the newspapers was sometimes intense, with local librarians reporting outbreaks of fighting over job listings.

Mobility. For some, leaving town to find work ultimately may be the best or only solution, especially if the local labor market, like that in Youngstown in the early 1980s, has a labor surplus.

When asked if they were considering leaving Youngstown, one-half of the discouraged and unemployed indicated that they were. In both groups, those below 54 years of age, males, and those educated through high school or beyond were more likely to be considering a move. Marital status and race appeared to make no difference.

Those considering a move represent those most likely to be in the primary labor force: young, educated males. This group is the most employable one, in general, so considering a move might make sense for them.

The fact that marital status appears not to be a factor is puzzling. Ordinarily, labor economists assume that unmarried people are more mobile than married people, because the former have fewer local ties than the latter.

If all or most discouraged and unemployed workers were to flee a depressed local labor market, this would produce a large drop in the labor force. Their exodus would relieve the surplus labor of one community and might reduce labor shortages in others. It is one thing to say that one is willing to move, but it is another to do so. Do workers really move from surplus labor markets in large numbers?

Although the potential for migration exists, most laid-off workers remain close to home. Nationally, according to the 1984 CPS plant-closing supplement, about 8 percent of discouraged workers involved in plant closings from 1979 to 1984 moved to a different city or county to look for work or to take a different job. Among the unemployed, mobility was higher, at 13 percent. These percentages demonstrate that, despite expressed intentions, the jobless are pretty much bound to the areas where their jobs were lost.

Potential for Self-Employment. Individual entrepreneurship, especially in the formation of small businesses, has recently received fresh attention as a potential contribution to the job-generation process and an alternative route to reemployment for displaced workers and the unemployed generally (Vaughan, et al. 1984).[4]

Vaughan and Buss (1987), O'Neill (1986), and others have promoted the development of entrepreneurship among such groups as the welfare-dependent, working poor, and displaced workers as a way to reduce unemployment and dependency. Discouraged workers are among those who could benefit from efforts to promote entrepreneurship. How much entrepreneurial experience do discouraged workers have? In addition, what is their potential to be self-employed?

Discouraged workers nationally are not particularly entrepreneurial (see Table 7.5). Less than 5 percent owned a small business before dropping out of the labor force, according to the SIPP survey. In Youngstown, discouraged workers, and unemployed people as well, like those nationally, had no small business experience: only one in ten had started a new business over the past decade. Only one in 20 Youngstown discouraged workers had invested in a new business, while only one in ten had ever worked for a start-up company.

Although discouraged workers may not have demonstrated much entrepreneurial spirit, perhaps they have some potential. When asked directly, many of the discouraged and unemployed alike appeared favorably disposed toward forming a small business. One-half did not prefer working for large companies, and one-half went so far as to prefer being their own boss.

Fear of risk-taking and lack of knowledge about getting a business started are major impediments to self-employment for the discouraged and unemployed worker. One-third would never start a business because of the financial risks. Slightly fewer say that it would take too much time. Two-fifths say they do not have the necessary skills. Finally, more than one-half are unfamiliar with procedures for starting a business. All in all, there is little to suggest that many discouraged or unemployed workers are likely candidates for the rough-and-tumble, high-risk life of the entrepreneur.

Table 7.5

Entrepreneurship Potential: Youngstown Discouraged and Unemployed

Question:	Discouraged	Unemployed
Prefer to work for large, established employer than start business		
Strongly agree	7.9	10.9
Agree	36.5	43.7
Disagree	49.2	38.8
Strongly disagree	6.3	6.6
Rather be boss than work for someone else		
Strongly agree	12.7	11.0
Agree	38.1	46.7
Disagree	46.0	41.2
Strongly disagree	3.2	1.1
Never start own business because of risks		
Strongly agree	4.8	7.0
Agree	30.6	33.3
Disagree	61.3	54.8
Strongly disagree	3.2	4.8
Always wanted to start a small business		
Strongly agree	8.1	11.9
Agree	40.3	40.0
Disagree	48.4	44.9
Strongly disagree	3.2	3.2
Running my own business would take too much time		
Strongly agree	1.6	3.3
Agree	19.0	29.9
Disagree	73.0	60.3
Strongly disagree	6.3	6.5
Don't have skills to start own business		
Strongly agree	4.8	2.7
Agree	36.5	39.2
Disagree	54.0	50.0
Strongly disagree	4.8	8.1
I am familiar with procedures for starting a small business		
Strongly agree	1.4	3.8
Agree	43.5	38.0
Disagree	48.4	52.7
Strongly disagree	6.5	4.9
In the past ten years:		
Attempted to start small business	7.9	13.5
Invested in someone else's small business	3.2	7.6
Worked for someone starting small business	11.1	17.8
N	102	128

Source: 1985 Youngstown Labor Market Follow-up Survey.

CONCLUSION

Despite the expressed desire of discouraged workers to find jobs, other evidence suggests that many are not highly motivated to work or to search for work. Others have little or no stable work experience or have held work demanding little in the way of education or training. In most respects, however, the discouraged worker population is not distinctive from the larger group of unemployed workers. In both groups, a large majority are prevented from holding highly rewarding jobs because they do not possess qualities that would readily qualify them for those jobs or that would make it easy for them to find or keep those jobs. In both groups, relatively few are prepared to search far and wide for any job or to aggressively pursue training and education opportunities.

A clearer picture of what discouraged workers need to achieve their expressed desires to work will emerge in chapter 8, when the group is subdivided.

NOTES

1. The jobs held by unemployed workers required about the same qualifications (as reported by respondents) as those held by discouraged workers.

2. The high percentage of displaced workers who were reemployed following participation in a training program does not imply that those programs are, in fact, successful in getting people back to work. Several things may account for this. First, some workers took training in fields that differed from those in which they got jobs. Second, many may have obtained jobs, often the same jobs, without having taken the training. Third, some workers took training, entered low-paying, entry-level jobs, and eventually quit, perhaps suggesting that some training is inappropriate. These and related issues are discussed by Buss and Vaughan (1988).

3. In Youngstown, participation rates were higher than the national level: five discouraged workers of the 85 interviewed indicated that they took retraining. Of the five, two were displaced and three were "other job losers." Although sub-samples for the unemployed were much larger, participation rates in training were about the same: 25 of 152 displaced and 24 of 209 other-job-loss unemployed persons attended training programs. The small number of displaced discouraged workers generally, coupled with the small percentage of those who attend retraining programs, may explain why the national CPS sampling procedure failed to turn up any cases for analysis. The probability of finding displaced discouraged worker trainees was just too low.

4. Small businesses (firms employing less than 20 workers) account for about 85 percent of all firms.

PART III
PUBLIC POLICY

8 *WHAT ARE THEIR NEEDS?*

The discouraged worker is not necessarily someone who has given up looking for work after repeated frustration, as most people had assumed. At the same time, the evidence indicates that many discouraged workers want to work; indeed they need to work but cannot.

Before we can properly analyze the implications of these observations for public policy, we need to take an additional step. In this chapter, discouraged workers are divided into need groups on the basis of what prevents them from being employed. This classification is useful for deciding what, if anything, the public sector can properly do to make them income-earning, productive workers.

A MORE DIFFERENTIATED PICTURE

Within the constraints imposed by the limited set of Bureau of Labor Statistics (BLS) survey questions and responses, it is possible to separate out two groups of discouraged workers who pose special problems (see Table 8.1). One is a group that either does not intend to look for work in the next year or, when asked directly, "Do you want a regular job now—either full- or part-time?" says no or "maybe—it depends." Among the discouraged, these are the least strongly attached to the labor force and most resemble the newer view of the discouraged. However, in 1984, only 19 percent of the discouraged workers responded to one or both questions in this manner. For convenience, we can label them the "detached" discouraged.

The second group whose responses differentiate them from other discouraged workers are those who face one or more clearly identifiable barriers to employ-

Table 8.1

Demographic Characteristics of Three Groups of Discouraged Workers (as percentages)

	All Discouraged Workers	Detached	Handicapped	Others
Single men under 25	14.6	25.1	13.3	12.1
Single women under 25	15.0	2.5	9.7	19.4
Married men	16.5	23.5	24.0	13.2
Married women	31.5	24.9	37.0	32.2
Singles 25 and over	22.3	24.1	16.1	23.2
Under 25	35.7	32.4	34.2	38.6
25-29	50.8	41.0	39.2	55.9
60 and older	13.5	26.6	26.6	5.5
White	65.2	67.8	73.2	62.9
Black	29.8	27.5	17.2	32.9
Other	5.0	4.7	9.5	4.2
Less than high school education	43.0	39.4	81.7	34.2
High school graduate	39.8	40.6	9.9	45.0
Some college or above	17.2	19.6	8.4	20.8
Male	39.1	53.3	42.7	34.3
Female	60.9	46.7	57.3	65.7
Last worked:				
Within 2 years	47.2	24.8	49.4	53.2
2-5 years ago	17.9	12.7	23.0	18.4
Over 5 years ago	17.4	37.7	17.3	11.6
Never	17.5	24.8	10.4	16.8

Source: 1984 CPS.

ment and cite these as reasons why they are not looking for work. They include people who have less than 12 years of education and cite lack of necessary schooling or training; those who are younger than 20 or older than 55, or who left a job due to retirement or old age, and claim that employers think they are too young or too old; and those that left a job for personal reasons (not including health) and cite personal handicaps (other than health) as reasons for not looking. Within the limits of the BLS question format, this helps to identify at least some of those who may have had, or could reasonably expect to have, unusual difficulty in getting work. In 1984, only 13 percent of all discouraged workers faced such identifiable barriers to employment. For convenience, we will label them the "personally handicapped" discouraged.

The remaining two-thirds of the discouraged are not so easily characterized. All we can say with these data is that they show more interest in working than the detached discouraged and do not claim to face the kinds of personal problems named by the handicapped discouraged. Despite the crudeness of this classification scheme, however, it becomes a tool with which we can look beyond the stereotypes and begin to assemble a more complex picture of what discouraged workers need to become more productively employed.

Those who show less commitment to working, that is, are detached, do have a distinct profile. Whereas the majority of all discouraged workers are female, a majority of the detached subgroup is male.

In fact, one-fourth of the detached are single males under the age of 25, a proportion roughly double that of the other subgroups. Their detachment is not simply a function of their youth and single status, however, since hardly any single women under the age of 25 are in this group. Nor is detachment related to race or education. In addition, while young single men are overrepresented among the detached, nearly equal proportions are married women, married men, and singles aged 25 years and over. Thus, even this narrowly defined subgroup of the discouraged defies stereotyping.

Discouraged workers who are handicapped by being too young, too old, or lacking in education are similarly diverse. Most obviously, they are much more likely than others to have less than a high school education, which is consistent with the way this category is defined. However, compared with other discouraged workers, they do *not* include disproportionate numbers of blacks and females—two groups generally viewed as handicapped in the job market due to lack of adequate schooling and training. One-third of the handicapped discouraged are under 25 years old. The group contains higher-than-average percentages of both married men and married women, and the lowest proportion of people who have never worked.

All in all, this initial attempt to sharpen the picture of discouragement by separating out subgroups of detached and personally handicapped serves mainly to suggest the limits of a classification based solely on the BLS survey protocol. To the extent that the two subgroups have distinctive demographic profiles, however, this exercise serves also to reemphasize the complexity of the phenomenon being examined and the pitfalls of the usual stereotypical thinking about discouraged workers.

ANOTHER DIMENSION

The labor-force attachment of discouraged or unemployed workers can be measured by their declared intentions to look for work or take a job, or by their recent efforts to find jobs. It can also be measured by the length of time that has passed since the individual last worked, or as the BLS asks the question, last worked "for pay at a regular job or business, either full-time or part-time." Of the national sample of discouraged workers, 29.8 percent have not worked in over two years and another 17.5 percent have never worked (see Table 8.2). Thus, a majority has not been employed within the last two years. The prolonged lack of contact with the world of work, whether or not it induces or indicates a loss of desire for work, can make it objectively more difficult to regain employment for a variety of reasons.

Table 8.2

Discouraged Workers Classified by Type of Discouragement and Length of Time since Last Regular Job: Percent of All Discouraged in Each Category

```
*********************************************************************
 Type of               _____Time Since Last Job_____    Never
Discouragement:        1+ Years    2-5 Years    5+ Years   Worked    Totals
---------------------------------------------------------------------

Detached                 4.8          2.5          7.3       4.8      19.4

Handicapped              6.5          3.0          2.3       1.4      13.2

Other                   35.9         12.4          7.8      11.3      67.5

Totals                  47.2         12.4         17.4      17.5     100.0
*********************************************************************
```

Source: 1984 CPS.

We would expect to find a correlation between detachment as measured by job-search behavior or declared intention and as measured by length of time out of work, and we do. Of the detached subgroup, about one-fourth have worked within the last two years. In fact, well over one-half either have not worked for over five years or have never worked. But, of both the personally handicapped group and the other discouraged, roughly one-half have been employed as recently as two years ago.

For purposes of further analysis, it may make sense to combine these two dimensions of labor-force attachment, intention and time, into a single measure. The heavy black outline around six cells in Table 8.2 includes a group, constituting 29.5 percent of all discouraged workers, who are only remotely attached to the labor force. We will refer to them as *"disconnected"* to distinguish them from the subset who were previously labeled as detached. Their distance from the world of employment, in time and/or intentions, is such that reinvolving them may be exceptionally difficult or costly.

Another, smaller group of discouraged workers have never worked, but have looked for work or at least declared their intentions to do so soon. Of the national sample, 12.7 percent are in this group, which is designated by the thinner outline in Table 8.2. Although evidently more motivated than the first group, their total lack of work experience also implies that efforts to get them into jobs could prove difficult and costly. We will refer to them as *"never connected."*

On the other hand, the remaining group of discouraged workers—the majority—has worked, often fairly recently, and has looked for work recently or intends to do so soon. They are much closer to the world of work. Although some may be handicapped by lack of preparation or in other ways, it seems reasonable to assume that in many instances they may be returned to work by methods that differ little from those used to help the officially unemployed.

Table 8.3

Youngstown Area Discouraged Workers Classified by Type of Discouragement and Length of Time Since Last Regular Job: Percent of All Discouraged in Each Category

Type of Discouragement:	Time Since Last Job			Never Worked	Totals
	1+ Years	2-5 Years	5+ Years		
Detached	9.4	5.8	10.5	10.5	36.2
Handicapped	2.3	0.0	1.2	2.3	5.8
Other	14.0	11.7	18.6	14.0	58.3
Totals	25.7	17.5	30.3	26.8	100.3

Source: 1984 CPS.

Note: Total exceeds 100.0 due to rounding.

CLASSIFYING THE YOUNGSTOWN AREA DISCOURAGED

The same classification scheme can be applied to discouraged workers in the Youngstown area (see Table 8.3). Given the already noted characteristics of that old steel-making region—the extensive disruption of established work patterns, the older industrial labor force, and the relative population stability—it would be no surprise if the needs profile of discouraged workers there was different from the national profile. This is, in fact, the case.

Youngstown area discouraged workers are more removed from the working world, on the average, both in time and psychological distance. Thirty percent of the Ohio workers have been out of work at least five years, compared with 17 percent nationally. Another 27 percent of Youngstown's discouraged have never worked, which again is a much higher proportion than the national level. In terms of intentions, 36 percent of discouraged workers in the Youngstown area either do not intend to look for work in the next year or are hesitant about wanting a regular job now. Again, this is a much higher proportion than the 19 percent in the national sample who have been labeled detached.

Putting the two dimensions together, fully 56 percent of the Youngstown discouraged could be regarded as *disconnected*, nearly twice the national proportion (see Table 8.4). The proportion of those "*never connected*" also is higher in the Ohio than in the U.S. sample. All in all, this evidence suggests that reinvolving the typical discouraged worker in a depressed labor market like Youngstown could prove to be more costly and difficult than in other places. Indeed, this difference may prove to be a defining characteristic of depressed labor markets.

Table 8.4

Comparison of Youngstown and National Samples: Proportions of Discouraged Workers in Three Need Groups (as percentages)

```
********************************************************************************
 Type of
Discouragement:            National Sample            Youngstown Area Sample
--------------------------------------------------------------------------------

Disconnected                   29.5                         56.0

Never Connected                12.7                         16.3

All Others                     57.8                         28.0

Total                         100.0                        100.3

********************************************************************************
```

Source: 1984 CPS and 1984 Youngstown Unemployment Rate Study.

Note: Total exceeds 100.0 due to rounding.

CONCLUSION

The needs classification developed in this chapter reflects our conviction that, for purposes of policy development, the critical information about a discouraged worker is how far removed he or she is, in terms of time and experience, from the working world. This classification is necessarily crude, given the limited survey information available, but it illustrates the insights available from a disaggregated look at the discouraged as well as other marginal workers. In the final chapter, this fresh and more detailed perspective on discouraged workers forms the basis for some suggestions concerning public policies to address the needs of people who say they want to work but cannot find jobs.

9 *HOW SHOULD THEY BE HELPED?*

A more complete, more accurate picture of discouraged workers provides us with the opportunity to suggest new directions for public policies addressed to their needs. What we have learned has broader implications as well, for employment and training policies to aid other people on the margin of the nation's labor force.

The first section of this final chapter addresses the way in which government defines and measures labor-force status; this issue has a direct immediate impact on who is offered various kinds of assistance. The second section examines what can be done to deal with discouragement, including the following: (1) deciding who should be helped; (2) what kinds of help are likely to be effective for various groups; and (3) under what conditions it makes economic sense for the government to invest in marginal workers. We conclude with a brief discussion of the broader economic effects of helping marginal workers.

DEFINITIONS AND STEREOTYPES

It makes little sense to continue thinking of discouraged workers as a distinct category. Increases or decreases in the number of people not looking for jobs because they believe that work is hard to find or employers will not hire them, will remain—along with unemployment rates—a useful indicator of cyclical changes in labor-market conditions. However, the "discouraged" label is too misleading, the group too heterogeneous, and its overlap with other, more meaningful categories too extensive for us to regard it as a meaningful labor-force category when planning public programs.

Rather than define labor-force groups only in terms of their recent labor-market behavior and their expression of intent, it would be wiser, in terms of guidance in policy development, to use more enduring characteristics that are predictive of *future* labor market success, with or without assistance.

This perspective is reinforced by recent research on poverty populations and the unemployed that presents a much more dynamic picture of these groups (Duncan 1984). How much sense does it make to talk about the poor as a static category, for instance, when people move in and out of poverty quite frequently? Over the decade from 1969 to 1978, 24 percent of the U.S. population fell below the federal poverty line for one or more years, but fewer than 1 percent were poor during the entire decade. Similarly, our best evidence regarding the dynamics of discouragement suggests that for a large majority this is a transient status. Yet when someone crosses the definitional boundary into or out of discouraged worker status, he or she does not gain or lose any personal attributes or assets that affect future employment earnings.

As an alternative to the categories currently used as a basis for conceptualizing labor-force status, we suggest that the nation's potential work force be arrayed along a dimension that might be called "distance to work." This may sound like a term to describe commuting patterns, but as used here, it refers to both the psychological and educational distance an individual must travel to be a likely candidate for productive steady employment. The psychological component is moderately correlated with the time that has passed since the person last worked. The educational component is related not only to schooling and skills training, but also to work-related abilities that are not necessarily the product of formal preparation. Placing people accurately on the distance-to-work dimension is a critical first step in determining what kinds of help they need to be mainstream workers and, indeed, whether such help is appropriate.

How can this dimension be applied to what we know about discouraged workers? The classifications developed in the preceding chapter indicate that both the "disconnected" and "never connected" subgroups of the discouraged must travel a greater distance to work, i.e., will need more preparation, than other discouraged workers. Within each subgroup, those with less education generally have the farthest to go.

From this follows our first public policy recommendation:

1. *Change the way labor-force status is measured.* The federal government should consider revising its basic approach to defining and measuring labor-force categories. The revised classifications should be based primarily on enduring individual characteristics that are likely to determine future employment and earnings prospects, thus providing a better guide for policy development and program administration.

STRATEGIES FOR MARGINAL WORKERS

In the United States at the end of the 1980s, all public policy discussion is cramped by sharpened awareness of fiscal limits and the intensified challenge of foreign economic competition. Efforts to bring marginal workers into the labor force will be impossible to justify unless they are seen as likely to pay for themselves by making the entire economy more productive and competitive.

From the government's standpoint, the most cost-effective programs will be those that target a *subset* of all marginal workers: first, those who otherwise would remain unproductive and continue to receive government transfer payments for months or perhaps years to come; and second, *within this group*, those who can be aided at reasonable expense, i.e., for whom the cost of assistance to society is more than offset by society's future gains.

Two problems are likely to limit the success of that targeting, however. One difficulty is the direct correlation between the likelihood of long-term dependency and the public cost of preparation for rewarding employment. Employing the distance-to-work notion, those who have the farthest to travel in terms of education, skill development, and work orientation will require more extensive, and therefore more costly, preparation. These also are the people most likely to become financially dependent for much of their lives on the work of others— either their relatives or taxpayers. Not only will the cost per worker rise as we address the needs of those who have the farthest to go, but also there will be a residual group for whom the cost will be prohibitively high (see Figure 9.1).

One should not immediately despair, however, because an evaluation of programs, such as the Job Corps, which emphasize long-term, costly preparation of high school dropouts, shows that those programs can be cost-effective. Although a one-year Job Corps slot cost over $13,000 in 1980—much more than ordinary classroom or on-the-job training—and dealt with what one writer calls "the hardest of the hard core," the program nevertheless scored better on a cost-benefit basis than less intensive, less ambitious programs (Glazer 1986). Among the major savings to society was reduced criminal activity among the participants (Taggart 1981).

A second problem in targeting resources to those marginal workers who can be helped at reasonable expense is the difficulty of identifying those people, within the targeted group, who will respond successfully to specific forms of help. In Figure 9.1, the shaded band around the heavy line indicating the average cost of assistance is meant to suggest that, within any group having apparently similar work preparation and attitudes, cost will vary over a wide range, depending on other characteristics of the individual (such as native ability and commitment) and the extent to which the specific program addresses the individual's specific needs. To use public resources wisely, people must be screened for their relative ability to benefit from the program, and for their competence and motivation.

Figure 9.1
Hypothesized Relationship between Cost of Helping and Distance to Work

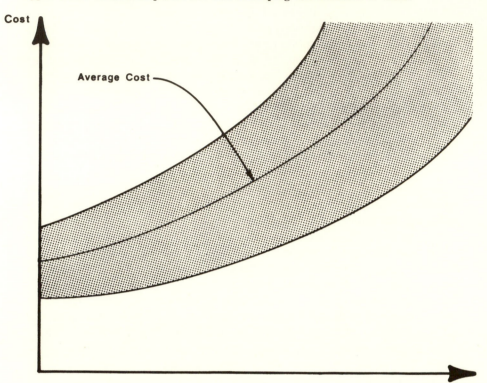

The implication of that type of cost-benefit perspective, combined with the distance-to-work notion, is that we should not necessarily concentrate on those who have the least distance to travel before they are prepared to work, although this strategy would minimize the average program cost per participant. Rather, we should develop an array of programs for the whole range of potential participants, from those who need minimal preparation to those who need intensive and prolonged education and resocialization. Then we should sort people carefully at each level of need so that resources are concentrated on those who can and will use them.

How does this perspective apply to discouraged workers and others who are marginal to the labor force? At the most general level, the very wide range of needs within the discouraged group suggests that rather than develop programs aimed at discouraged workers in particular, governments should develop and deliver an array of programs for all marginal workers, not excluding those who are now marginally employed, and then sort people into programs according to the degree of preparation needed for stable employment. Since, nationally, a large number of discouraged workers are far removed in time and psychological distance from working life, helping them would require relatively expensive programs. Those with other deficiencies, such as inadequate or incomplete schooling, will require still greater outlays. Those costs can only be justified for individuals whose behavior demonstrates competence and motivation, suggesting that they could absorb and respond to help.

If the goal is to maximize society's benefits from public expenditures to prepare marginal workers for employment, then one additional selection filter must be applied. Limited resources should be directed first to younger workers, especially those who would otherwise be likely to depend on public support or crime for their income. The benefits of redirecting a young person from a life of dependency or criminal activity to one of productive contributions are so great that they tend to overwhelm questions of relative cost. At the other extreme, society benefits far less from the brief reemployment of a person near the age of retirement. In the latter case, relative cost must be the main issue in deciding whether to provide help.

From this analysis, our second and third policy recommendations follow:

2. *Design programs around need for work preparation.* An array of programs should be provided to meet a range of needs, from minimal preparation to long-term remediation and resocialization. Programs should be available to all marginal workers, regardless of their current employment status, and should not specifically be directed at discouraged workers.

3. *Screen for competence, motivation, and likely long-term benefits.* Programs at each need level can be cost-effective, but only if participants are carefully screened to concentrate resources on those who are able and willing to benefit and are likely to provide the greatest net social return from lifelong productive employment.

MARGINAL WORKERS AND WELFARE REFORM

To better appreciate what should be done for discouraged workers, this question should be set in the broader context of the recently renewed debate over U.S. employment and welfare policies. A great deal of the new attention given in the 1980s to welfare reform and the problems of the "underclass" has focused on one question: What will it take to reduce the numbers of people who are chronically dependent on public assistance and put them to work?

This seemingly straightforward policy goal has two very different possible meanings. In fact, the debate between those who stress work requirements and those who stress work preparation and support is seemingly one about *means*, but it is really an obscurely conducted debate about *ends*.

The policy discussion would be conducted in clearer terms if the discussants would recognize that reducing dependency can mean one of two things:

- *Cycling*: limiting the length of spells of not working, and thus dependency, and the debilitating hardship and cumulative damage to people that
  long-term dependency produces; or

- *Development*: investing in people to enchance their employability,
  thereby increasing the economic rewards of work to the point that they
  surpass those of idleness.

Although either policy goal may be justified where benefits exceed costs, the
two goals clearly imply different programs. Those who push primarily for work
requirements implicitly are advocating churning or cycling as an end in itself.
If unemployment is progressively debilitating and long-term dependency is devastating in terms of its impact on individuals and family life, then breaking these
spells, even intermittently, may be a worthy goal. The careful evaluations conducted by the Manpower Development Research Corporation (MDRC) show that
some relatively low-cost work programs benefit both welfare recipients and
taxpayers by producing increases in earnings and employment and decreases in
welfare dependency (Gueron 1987).

If the programs pay for themselves, even by narrowly defined measures of
cost-effectiveness, they are desirable for at least part of the dependent population
and presumably for others who are marginal to the labor force and at risk of
dependency. However, it should also be clear that these programs do very little
to advance the economic status and alleviate the hardship of participants in the
short run; in the state programs surveyed by MDRC, employment rates for
participants rose, on the average, between 3 and 8 percent, which produced
gains in earnings (not in household income) of between 8 and 37 percent (Gueron
1987). Moreover, those programs have no substantial impact on earnings and
employment in the long run. Again, the MDRC findings suggest that:

> While these sorts of programs are successful in increasing the employment
> and earnings of welfare recipients, they are not likely to allay employers'
> concerns about the skills gaps or the lack of basic skills in the emerging
> labor force. Nor should we look to these relatively low-cost, low intensity
> programs, by themselves to solve the problems of poverty and dependency.
> (Gueron 1987, p. 12.)

Other people push for training, remedial education, child care, extending
Medicaid coverage during the transition to employment, and other preparation
and support. They are really advocating a different, more ambitious goal than
those who favor work requirements alone. Their ambition is to draw people
permanently from the economic shallows into the productive mainstream. This
requires not merely finding a job but holding it over time and earning a good
wage. If the individual is to have an economic incentive to make this difficult
transition, the wage, combined with transitional public (usually noncash) support,

should exceed what a marginal worker could ordinarily command. The goal is to leapfrog the stratum of dead-end, near-minimum-wage jobs to the stratum that provides not only higher wages, but also opportunities for advancement and important nonwage benefits.

Programs that help people achieve this goal are bound to be far more expensive than cycling efforts, but they also offer greater social benefits. It is an open question, but one worth careful study, whether well-designed development programs benefit significant numbers of people at a justifiable cost. In addition to the Job Corps evaluation mentioned earlier, evidence from MDRC's long-term follow-up study of participants in a Baltimore, Maryland, program suggests that "education and training may have delayed but increasing payoffs," and that "more intensive programs may be required if programs are to reach the multi-problem, longest-term [welfare] recipients" (Gueron 1987, pp. 12–13).

When reframed in these terms, the debate over welfare reform offers insights applicable to discouraged workers. We know that the young people in this category who have never worked, by and large, have very limited employment and career prospects (Bane and Ellwood 1983). Most will remain on the margins, unless they receive substantial publicly sponsored investments to make them good candidates for good jobs. The same is apparently true for many discouraged workers whose previous work efforts yielded little in return and whose limited education and training probably restrict them to low-skill jobs. On the other hand, we know that many of the same people evidence only a limited desire to work. We surmise, but cannot establish from the evidence available, that many also have limiting mental and physical conditions.

The divergence of immediate employment potential within the discouraged worker population, combined with the dual policy goals discussed earlier, implies a two-channel approach to programs for discouraged workers. One group—those who need extensive investment and demonstrate the capacity and motivation to use it—should be offered high-cost *developmental* programs. The core of these programs must be intensive, often prolonged, educational remediation and employment-skills training. The transition to work must be supported by an individually tailored package of supports, including subsidies for housing, health care, child care, and transportation. However, it must be made clear to participants that these temporary work-related nonentitlement benefits are contingent upon continued progress toward stable employment and will be withdrawn from those who fail to perform. This provides the correct incentives for work effort and makes the best use of public dollars. Supports should be phased out as participants increase their earnings, but the combined tax rate on effective income for withdrawing entitlement and nonentitlement benefits must not be so high that continued work effort appears to offer no economic benefit.

The second group—those with similar needs but lacking capacity or motivation, plus those already possessing the education, skills, and other attributes required for mainstream employment—should be channeled into lower-cost *cycling* programs, including required work as a condition for receiving public assistance. Communities where private entry-level job opportunities are in short supply should set up community work-experience programs, so that every person who is able to work does so.

This two-track program structure would ensure that discouraged workers in each group receive maximum benefits and that scarce public resources are conserved.

The remainder of the discouraged worker population would receive no special help. They include people not dependent on public assistance whose earning capacity has been demonstrated but who have little desire to work or whose preconditions for work are so restrictive that they cannot easily be satisfied in the local labor market. Many in this group, while still young enough to work, have retired, whether voluntarily or not, from regular employment and have no great economic need to work. Not assisting those people does not constitute any sort of moral judgment on them, but rather an economic judgment that the public expenditure would not be justified.

To summarize, while not favoring separate programs for discouraged workers, we do recommend that two-program channels be developed for discouraged workers, as well as others dependent or potentially dependent on public assistance. Our next policy recommendation, therefore, is:

4. *Create a two-channel program structure.* Provide intensive developmental help for one group of discouraged workers, limited help to a second, and no help to the remainder, thus maximizing the benefits to all and spending scarce public resources in the most efficient possible manner.

CREATING JOB OPPORTUNITIES

An employment strategy for marginal workers that focuses just on remedying the failings of individuals is one-sided. It would be easy to sidestep discussion of the need to create job opportunities by placing this problem beyond the scope of the present study or by pointing to government-sponsored projections that a shortage of skilled workers will emerge by the turn of the century. Unfortunately, policymakers, those who want work, and others who live in the real world of immediate problems must be concerned with both sides of the employment equation. When people are prepared for jobs, the jobs must be ready for them. Unless both problems are addressed, employment policies fail.

Research on the growth of the underclass in American cities has found that it is rooted in a mismatch between the kinds of jobs available in urban labor markets and the skills of those who live there (Wilson 1987). During the decades when blacks from the rural South and those fleeing poverty in Latin America and the Caribbean were becoming the dominant groups in urban ghettos, the economic structure of U.S. cities was changing due to the elimination of the kinds of entry-level jobs that were the traditional stepping stones by which immigrants advanced to the middle class. Into the economic void poured alcohol and drug addiction, crime, teenage pregnancy, and all of the other social pathologies—nameable and unnamed—that are embodied by the underclass.

Solutions to this problem must begin with the public education system and continue with the kinds of intensive remedial investments that we have suggested are appropriate for the fraction of marginal workers who would otherwise be long-term dependents and have the capacity and motivation needed to make such investments pay off. Yet the full benefit of educational and remedial programs will not be realized unless they are followed by publicly or privately sponsored efforts to ensure that participants get good jobs. Employers need economic incentives to hire, retain, and continue training people rescued from the economic margin. In the absence of labor shortages, this requires some form of government subsidy. Those subsidies can take many forms. Employment vouchers have some advantages over other subsidy mechanisms; they should be restricted to those in whom the public has already made the greatest investment and to situations where employers would not otherwise hire such workers (Vaughan and Buss 1987). Therefore, our final policy recommendation is:

5. *Assist employers willing to hire and retain graduates of development programs*. Government should provide subsidies to private employers who otherwise would not be in a position to hire, retain, and continue to train discouraged workers who have successfully completed development programs.

CONCLUSION

Discouraged workers are not what the name implies. Indeed, the complex portrait of these workers that emerges from a closer look at this group shows such diversity that a single label has little or no utility.

New insights on employment policy can be gained by abandoning both this particular label and the near-exclusive use of current employment status, by both government and academic researchers, to describe the labor market. Most people at the margins of the labor force continually move from employment to unemployment, to being out of the labor force and back again. Background characteristics are more stable and are keys to determining what people need and the public programs most likely to help them.

The recommendations in this chapter would aid both those classified as discouraged and other marginal workers. To use scarce public resources where they will have the greatest impact, program designers and administrators must distinguish those who can benefit from intensive and costly development programs from those who would be better served by less expensive cycling into entry-level employment, and those for whom employment assistance is either not necessary or not worth the expenditure of public funds.

Efforts to treat the individual problems of discouraged workers will not be as effective as they should be unless we also address the structural features of labor markets that isolate those living in the urban ghetto and others on the social margins from stable rewarding employment. Where and when labor is in short supply, we can expect private employers to hire marginal workers and provide them with the opportunities for promotion into mainstream jobs. At other times, government must provide subsidies to employers who create those opportunities.

President Reagan, looking at the long lists of job ads in the newspapers, once suggested that many of the unemployed are people not eager to work. Speaker O'Neill responded that, by failing to provide jobs to people who want to work, the nation was wasting its human resources. Neither argument comes to grips with the difficult task of designing cost-effective public programs for marginal workers and creating job opportunities to use the people who want to work, need to work, can be productive workers, but will otherwise never hold good jobs. We recognize the difficulty of developing those policies, but we refuse to be discouraged.

BIBLIOGRAPHY

Alban, Edward, and Jackson, Mark. "The Job Vacancy-Unemployment Ratio and Labor-Force Participation." *Industrial and Labor Relations Review* 29 (1976): 412–419.

Bane, Mary Joe, and Ellwood, David T. *The Dynamics of Dependence: The Routes to Self-Sufficiency*. Cambridge, Mass.: Urban Systems Research and Engineering, Inc., 1983.

Barth, Peter S. "Unemployment and Labor Force Participation." *Southern Economic Journal* 34 (1968): 375–383.

Bickert, Tony. "The Duck Man." *Pittsburgh Magazine*, March 1986, p. 120.

Bowen, William G., and Finegan, T. A. "Labor Force Participation and Unemployment." In *Employment Policy and the Labor Market*, edited by Arthur M. Ross. Berkeley: University of California Press, 1965.

Bradburn, N. M. *The Structure of Psychological Well-Being*. Chicago: Aldine, 1969.

Bradbury, Katharine L. "Prospects for Growth in New England: The Labor Force." *New England Economic Review*, September–October 1985, pp. 50–60.

Bradbury, Katharine L., and Browne, Lynn E. "Black Men in the Labor Market." *New England Economic Review*, March–April 1986, pp. 32–42.

Browne, Lynn E. "Structural Change and Dislocated Workers." *New England Economic Review*, January–February 1985, pp. 15–27.

Buss, Terry F. "Assessing the Accuracy of Bureau of Labor Statistics Monthly Unemployment Rates: A Case Study of the Youngstown/Warren SMSA." *Industrial and Labor Relations Review* 39 (1986a): 241–250.

Buss, Terry F. "Local Area Unemployment Rates and Their Implications for Human Resource Planning." *Journal of Economic and Social Measurement* 14 (1986b): 1–18.

Buss, Terry F., and Redburn, F. Stevens. *Shutdown at Youngstown: Public Policy for Mass Unemployment*. Albany: State University of New York Press, 1983.

Buss, Terry F, and Redburn, F. Stevens. "Psychological Well-Being of Workers in Distressed Communities." *Location and Stigma*, edited by Christopher Smith and John Gibbs. London: George Allen and Unwin, 1986a.

Buss, Terry F., and Redburn, F. Stevens. *Reemployment after a Shutdown: The Closing of Youngstown Sheet and Tube, 1977 to 1985*. Columbus: Ohio Bureau of Employment Services, 1986b.

Buss, Terry F. and Redburn, F. Stevens. "Plant Closings: Impacts and Responses." *Economic Development Quarterly* 1 (1987): 170–177.

Buss, Terry F., and Roger J. Vaughan. *On the Rebound: A Human Services Response to Plant Closings*. Washington, D.C.: Council of State Planning Agencies, 1988.

Cassimatis, Emanuel. "Mental Health Viewed as an Ideal." *Journal of Psychiatry* 42 (1979): 241–254.

Cave, George. "Job Rationing, Unemployment, and Discouraged Workers." *Journal of Labor Economics* 1 (1983): 286–306.

Danziger, Sheldon H., and Weinberg, D. H., eds. *Fighting Poverty: What Works and What Doesn't*. Cambridge, Mass.: Harvard University Press, 1986.

Domestic Policy Council on Low Income Opportunity. *Up from Dependence— A Report to the President*. Washington, D.C.: Domestic Policy Council, 1986.

Duggan, James E. "The Labor-Force Participation of Older Workers." *Industrial and Labor Relations Review* 37 (1984): 416–430.

Duncan, G. J. *Years of Poverty, Years of Plenty*. Ann Arbor: Institute for Social Research, University of Michigan, 1984.

Feldstein, Martin, and Poterba, James. "Unemployment Insurance and Reservation Wages." *Journal of Public Economics* 23 (1984): 141–167.

Finegan, Aldrich T. *The Measurement, Behavior, and Classification of Discouraged Workers*. Background Paper 12. Washington, D.C.: National Commission on Employment and Unemployment Statistics, 1978.

Finegan, Aldrich T. "Discouraged Workers and Economic Fluctuations." *Industrial and Labor Relations Review* 34 (1981): 88–102.

Flaim, Paul O. "Discouraged Workers and Changes in Unemployment." *Monthly Labor Review* 96 (1973): 8–16.

Flaim, Paul O. "Discouraged Workers: How Strong Are Their Links to the Job Market?" *Monthly Labor Review*, August 1984, pp. 8–11.

Flaim, Paul O., and Seghal, Ellen. "Displaced Workers of 1979–83: How Well They Fared." *Monthly Labor Review*, June 1985, pp. 3–16.

Garraty, John. *Unemployment in History*. New York: Free Press, 1978.

Gastwirth, Joseph L. "Estimating the Number of 'Hidden Unemployed.' " *Monthly Labor Review*, March 1973, pp. 16–26.

Gastwirth, Joseph L. "On the Decline of Male Labor Force Participation." *Monthly Labor Review*, October 1972, pp. 44–46.

Gellner, Christopher G. "Enlarging the Concept of a Labor Reserve." *Monthly Labor Review*, April 1975, pp. 20–28.

Gilroy, Curtis L. "Supplemental Measures of Labor Force Underutilization." *Monthly Labor Review*, May 1975, pp. 13–23.

Glazer, Nathan. "Education and Training Programs and Poverty." In *Fighting Poverty: What Works and What Doesn't*, edited by Sheldon Danziger and D. Weinberg. Cambridge, Mass.: Harvard University Press, 1986.

Goodwin, Leonard. *Do the Poor Want to Work?* Washington, D.C.: The Brookings Institution, 1972.

Grant, James H., and Hamermesh, Daniel S. "Labor Market Competition among Youths, White Women and Others." *Review of Economics and Statistics* 63 (1981): 354–60.

Gueron, Judith M. "Testimony before the Subcommittee on Education and Health of the Joint Economic Committee, U.S. Congress." Washington, D.C.: November 19, 1987.

Hamel, Harvey R. "Two-fifths of Discouraged Sought Work during Prior Six-Month Period." *Monthly Labor Review*, March 1979, pp. 58–60.

Hayes, John, and Nutman, Peter. *Understanding the Unemployed*. Tavistock Publications, 1981.

Hayghe, Howard. "Families and the Rise of Working Wives—An Overview." *Monthly Labor Review* 99 (1976): 12–19.

Healy, Robert. "Reagan, Jobs and the Jobless." Boston *Globe*, January 31, 1986.

Horkey, Margaretta. "Housewife Sees End of Dream for Americans." *The Vindicator*, February 23, 1986.

Horvath, Francis W. "The Pulse of Economic Change: Displaced Workers of 1981–1985." *Monthly Labor Review*, June 1987, pp. 3–12.

Howe, Wayne J. "Temporary Help Workers: Who They Are, What Jobs They Hold." *Monthly Labor Review*, November 1986, pp. 45–47.

Job, Barbara Cottman. "How Likely Are Individuals to Enter the Labor Force?" *Monthly Labor Review* 102 (1979): 28–34.

Johnston, Denis F., and Wetzel, James R. "Effect of the Census Undercount on Labor Force Estimates." *Monthly Labor Review*, March 1969, pp. 3–13.

Levitan, Sar, and Taggart, Robert. "Employment and Earnings Inadequacy: A Measure of Worker Welfare." *Monthly Labor Review*, October 1973, pp. 19–27.

Levitan, Sar; Magnum, Garth L.; and Marshall, Ray. *Human Resources and Labor Markets*. New York: Harper and Row, Inc., 1981.

Lerman, Robert I. "Unemployment among Low Income and Black Youth." *Youth and Society* 17 (1986): 237–266.

Lilla, Mark. "Why the 'Income Distribution' Is So Misleading." *Public Interest* (1986): 62–76.

Mallar, Charles. *Evaluation of the Impact of the Job Corps Program*. Princeton: Mathematica Policy Research, 1982.

Mead, Lawrence. *Beyond Entitlement*. New York: Free Press, 1986.

Meyer, David P. *Report on Underemployment from a Human Service Perspective*. Columbus: National Center for Research in Vocational Education, Ohio State University, 1985.

Miller, Herman P. "Measuring Subemployment in Poverty Areas of Large U.S. Cities." *Monthly Labor Review*, October 1973, pp. 10–18.

Mincer, Jacob. "Labor-Force Participation and Unemployment: A Review of Recent Evidence." In *Prosperity and Unemployment* edited by R. A. and M. S. Gordon. New York: John Wiley and Sons, Inc., 1966.

Mincer, Jacob. "Determining Who Are the Hidden Unemployed." *Monthly Labor Review*, March 1973, pp. 27–30.

Moynihan, Daniel P. *Family and Nation*. San Diego: Harcourt, Brace, Jovanovich, 1986.

Munnell, Alicia H. "Lessons from the Income Maintenance Experiments: An Overview." *New England Economic Review*, May–June 1987, pp. 32–45.

Murray, Charles. *Losing Ground: American Social Policy 1950–1980*. New York: Basic Books, 1984.

National Commission on Employment and Unemployment Statistics (NCEUS). *Counting the Labor Force*. Washington, D.C.: NCEUS, 1979.

National Institute of Mental Health. *Unemployment and Mental Health: A Report on Research Resources for Technical Assistance, Final Report*. Washington, D.C.: National Institute of Mental Health, 1985.

Natriello, Gary. *School Dropouts: Patterns and Policies*. New York: Teachers College Press, 1986.

Newman, Barry. " 'On the Dole': High Unemployment Wreaks Vast Changes on Life in Britain." *Wall Street Journal*, November 10, 1986.

Ondeck, Carol M. "Discouraged Workers' Link to Jobless Rate Reaffirmed." *Monthly Labor Review*, October 1978, pp. 40–42.

O'Neill, Hugh. *Creating Opportunity*. Washington, D.C.: Council of State Planning Agencies, 1985.

Parnes, Herbert S. "Labor Force Participation and Labor Mobility." *A Review of Industrial Relations Research* 1 (1970): 1–78.

Redburn, F. Stevens, and Buss, Terry F. *Responding to America's Homeless*. New York: Praeger, 1986.

Redburn, F. Stevens, and Buss, Terry F. "Religious Leaders and the Politics of Revitalization." In Robert Eyestone, ed., *Public Policy Formation*. Greenwich, Conn.: JAI Press, 1984.

Richards, Bill. "Down the Ladder. They Have Jobs Again in La Porte, but Work Doesn't Pay So Well." *Wall Street Journal*, March 3, 1986.

Rosenblum, Marc. "Discouraged Workers and Unemployment." *Monthly Labor Review*, September 1974, pp. 28–30.

Rosenfeld, Carl. "Job Search of the Unemployed, May 1976." *Monthly Labor Review*, November 1977, Appendix.

Schwab, Karen. "Early Labor-Force Withdrawal of Men Participants and Non-participants Aged 58–63." *Social Security Bulletin*, August 1974, pp. 24–33.

Schweitzer, Stuart O., and Smith, Ralph E. "The Persistence of the Discouraged Worker Effect." *Industrial and Labor Relations Review* 27 (1974): 249–260.

"The Shadow Economy: Grossly Deceptive Product." *The Economist*, September 19, 1987, pp. 25–28.

Shamir, Boas. "Protestant Work Ethic, Work Involvement and the Psychological Impact of Unemployment." *Journal of Occupational Behaviour* 7 (1986): 25–38.

Shiskin, Julius. "Employment and Unemployment: The Doughnut or the Hole?" *Monthly Labor Review*, February 1976, pp. 3–10.

Shiskin, Julius, and Stein, Robert L. "Problems in Measuring Unemployment." *Monthly Labor Review*, August 1975, pp. 3–10.

Stein, Herbert. "Still at Work on Full Employment." *Wall Street Journal*, February 13, 1986.

Stein, Robert L. "New Definitions for Employment and Unemployment." *Employment and Earnings*, February, 1967a, pp. 3–27.

Stein, Robert L. "Reasons for Non-Participation in the Labor Force," *Monthly Labor Review*, July 1967b, pp. 22–27.

Stevans, Lonnie K.; Register, Charles A.; and Grimes, Paul W. "The Labor Force Attachment of Discouraged Workers." *Work and Occupations* 14 (1987): 3–21.

Taggart, Robert. *A Fisherman's Guide: An Assessment of Training Strategies*. Kalamazoo: Upjohn Institute, 1981.

Tannenwald, Robert. "Why Has the Unemployment Rate Declined So Rapidly?" *New England Economic Review*, September–October 1984, pp. 34–38.

Tella, Alfred. "Labor Force Sensitivity to Employment by Age, Sex." *Industrial Relations* 4 (1965): 69–83.

U.S. Bureau of the Census. *The Current Population Survey*. Washington, D.C.: Department of Congress, 1978.

U.S. Congress, House Subcommittee on Government Operations. *Hearings on Counting All the Jobless*, 99th Cong. 2d sess., March 20, 1986a.

U.S. Congress, Office of Technology Assessment. *Technology and Structural Unemployment: Reemploying Displaced Adults*. Washington, D.C.: Government Printing Office, 1986b.

U.S. Department of Labor, Bureau of Labor Statistics. *Report on Displaced Workers 1979–83*. Bulletin 2240. Washington, D.C.: Government Printing Office, 1985.

U.S. General Accounting Office (U.S. GAO) *Noncash Benefits: Initial Results Show Valuation Methods Differentially Affect the Poor*. Washington, D.C.: U.S. GAO, October 1986a.

U.S. General Accounting Office (U.S. GAO). *Report on Dislocated Workers: Extent of Business Closures, Layoffs, and the Public and Private Response*. Washington, D.C.: U.S. GAO, 1986b.

Vaughan, Roger J., Robert Pollard, and Barbara Dyer. *The Wealth of States*. Washington, D.C.: Council of State Planning Agencies, 1984.

Vaughan, Roger J., and Terry F. Buss. *Reducing Poverty through Economic Development*. Columbus: Ohio Board of Regents, Urban University Program, 1987.

Veit, Clairice and Ware, John E. "The Structure of Psychological Distress and Well-Being in General Populations." *Journal of Consulting and Clinical Psychology*, 51(1983), pp. 730–742.

Vietorisz, T.; Meir, R.; and Giblin, J. "Subemployment: Exclusion and Inadequacy Indexes." *Monthly Labor Review*, May 1975, pp. 3–12.

Vroman, Wayne. "The Labor Force Reserve: A Re-estimate." *Industrial Relations* 9 (1970): 379–393.

Wachter, Michael L. "A Labor Supply Model for Secondary Workers." *Review of Economics and Statistics*, May 1972, pp. 141–151.

Ware, John E.; Johnson, S. A.; Davis-Avery, A.; and Brook, R. H. *Conceptualization and Measurement of Health–Vol. 1*. Santa Monica, Cal.: The Rand Corporation, 1979.

Warr, Peter. "A Study of Psychological Well-being." *British Journal of Psychology* 69(1978), pp. 111–121.

Warr, Peter and T. Wall. *Work and Well-being*. Harmondsworth: Penguin, 1975.

"Why Women Get Jobs." *Economist*, August 23, 1986.

Wilson, William J. *The Truly Disadvantaged: The Inner City, the Underclass, and Public Policy*. Chicago: University of Chicago Press, 1987.

Wool, Harold. *Discouraged Workers, Potential Workers, and National Employment Policy*. Special Report No. 24. Washington, D.C.: National Commission for Manpower Policy, June 1978.

INDEX

ABOUT THE AUTHORS

TERRY F. BUSS is a professor of urban studies and senior research associate at the Center for Urban Studies, The University of Akron. His latest books, coauthored with Roger J. Vaughan and published by the Council of State Planning Agencies, include: *On the Rebound: Developing a Human Service Response to Plant Closings* (1988), *A State Strategy for Preventing and Treating Rural Poverty* (1988), *Picking Up the Pieces: Economic Recovery After a Plant Closing* (1988). He is now working on a book about the working poor and welfare poor.

F. STEVENS REDBURN is an economist in the U.S. Office of Management and Budget in Washington, D.C. He is the co-author, with Terry Buss, of *Responding to America's Homeless* (Praeger, 1987) and *Revitalizing the U.S. Economy* (Praeger, 1987). He is currently working on banking and housing issues.